THE REFRACTIVE THINKER®

AN ANTHOLOGY OF
DOCTORAL WRITERS

VOLUME XVIII
Project Management
Strategies to Enhance
Workflow and Productivity

Edited by Dr. Cheryl A. Lentz

THE REFRACTIVE THINKER® PRESS

The Refractive Thinker®: An Anthology of Higher Learning
Vol. XVIII: Project Management: Strategies to Enhance Workflow and Productivity

The Refractive Thinker® Press
http://www.RefractiveThinker.com
https://Twitter.com/DrCherylLentz
https://www.Facebook.com/RefractiveThinker/

All rights reserved. No part of this book may be reproduced or transmitted in any form or by any means, graphic, electronic or mechanical, including photocopying, recording, taping, Web distribution, or by any informational storage and retrieval system without written permission from the publisher except for the inclusion of brief quotations in a review or scholarly reference.

Books are available through The Refractive Thinker® Press at special discounts for bulk purchases for the purpose of sales promotion, seminar attendance, or educational purposes. Special volumes can be created for specific purposes and to organizational specifications. Please contact us for further details.

Individual authors own the copyright to their individual materials.
The Refractive Thinker® Press has each author's permission to reprint.

Copyright © 2020 by The Refractive Thinker® Press
Managing Editor: Dr. Cheryl A. Lentz • DrCherylLentz@gmail.com

Library of Congress Control Number: 2013945437

ISBN: 978-1-7329382-6-7
*Kindle and electronic versions available

Refractive Thinker® logo by Joey Root; The Refractive Thinker® Press logo design by Jacqueline Teng; cover design and production by Gary A. Rosenberg.

10 9 8 7 6 5 4 3 2 1

Contents

Testimonials, v

FOREWORD
Andrew (Andy) Allen
Gratitude: The Pride of Workmanship, xi

Preface, xv

Acknowledgments, xix

CHAPTER 1
Dr. James Wright, Dr. Wendy Herrburger, Dr. Karen Balcanoff & Dr. Judie Brill
New and Emerging Tools and Trends in Project Management, 1

CHAPTER 2
Dr. Frank Musmar
Successful Project Management Strategies at Health Care Organizations, 23

CHAPTER 3
Dr. Aaron Armour & Dr. Avideh Sadaghiani-Tabrizi
Project Management's Considerations to Address Enterprise-wide Cyberthreats, 47

CHAPTER 4
Dr. Cynthia J. Young
Preventing Wastes of Project Costs and Schedules Using Purposeful Knowledge Management, 63

CHAPTER 5
Dr. Ivan Salaberrios
Defining Outsourcing and Offshoring, 83

CHAPTER 6
Dr. Alla Adams
Care Coordination Models in Accountable Care Organizations: Achievements, Challenges, and Opportunities, 111

CHAPTER 7
Dr. Gail Ade & Dr. Alan L. Bundschuh Jr.
Enhancing Group Dynamics and Project Success Through Situational Leadership Lens, 131

CHAPTER 8
Dr. Natalie Casale
Help Wanted: Strategies for Hiring Your Perfect Project Manager, 149

CHAPTER 9
Dr. Deji West
Project Management: The Stark Choice— Projectize or Stagnate, 167

CHAPTER 10
Dr. Amy Yoder, Dr. Yvonne Gonzalez, Dr. Teresa Sanders, & Dr. Cheryl Lentz
The Project Management— Impact of Educational Curriculum Design, 183

Index, 205

2020 Catalog, 207

Testimonials

Brian Jud

Executive Director of the Association of Publishers for Special Sales, author of 14 books including
How to Make Real Money Selling Books
http://www.bookmarketingworks.com/

Authors always want to know the latest out-of-the-box strategy to sell more of their books. *The Refractive Thinker®* series adopts this innovative-thinking approach, so you can get your doctoral research out of academia and into the hands of those who need it. This volume, specific to the field of project management is a particularly good example of how to make that happen regarding strategies to enhance workflow and productivity. There is no need to go it alone. Join your colleagues on a journey in search of innovative solutions as you navigate the landscape of business.

Clarissa Burt

CEO/Founder of In the Limelight
https://clarissaburt.com/
https://clarissaburt.com/magazine/

Learning doesn't always happen in a formal classroom; sometimes one learns from the school of hard knocks and experience. *The Refractive Thinker®* series looks to connecting these two worlds of business and learning in this volume regarding project management—the ability to focus on strategies for effective project outcomes. A refractive thinker is one who never settles for anything less than everything, daring to question what is, in favor of what might be. Dr. Cheryl Lentz dared to change the model of academic publishing by understanding the power of connection between education and business—to make research more accessible to business owners and entrepreneurs. No one benefits from playing small, particularly with one's personal passion in the world of knowledge. Refractive thinkers play on a big stage, truly desiring to change their world and ours. Join them.

Olivia Parr-Rud, MS

Data Scientist, Bestselling and Award-winning author, and Corporate Love Ambassador
https://www.LoveMakeItYourBusiness.com

To thrive in today's fast-paced, high-tech, global economy, companies must become more adaptable and resilient. This is especially true when it comes to project management because of its high sensitivity to ever changing technologies and shifting market demands. *The Refractive Thinker®* series offers powerful, practical insights and strategies for navigating our increasing complex business landscape. The blend of academic rigor with real world applications through the lens of refractive thinking strategies provides unique, cutting-edge solutions. *The Refractive Thinker® Vol XVIII: Project Management* is a potent addition to this series. Every business should make this entire series a staple in their corporate library.

Linda F. Patten

Leadership Trainer for Women Entrepreneurs and Changemakers, CEO of Dare2Lead with Linda
http://www.dare2leadwithlinda.com

As a trainer and project manager, I have been immersed in the literature around the best practices in the field. Having been schooled in rational project management, I understand the importance of defining the project, planning the project and implementing the project with all the steps that that entails. However, in today's world, there is a need for thinking that has no limits, and is not stuck in convention. The writers in this compilation are exceptional in their ability to challenge the status quo and to look beyond the steps of project management. While each of the chapters held my interest and caused me to examine my thoughts around their topic, I was especially drawn to the "Thoughts from the Academic Entrepreneur" at the end of each chapter. This compilation is priceless for those project managers today.

"The 'P' in PM is as much about 'people' management as it is about 'project' management."
—Cornelius Fichtner, PM

We had risen to probably one of the greatest challenges in history, put a man on the moon in the decade. We'd created incredible technologies. But what was most important, we'd created the teams, what I call the human factor. People who were energized by a mission.
—Gene Kranz, NASA Flight Director

FOREWORD
Gratitude:
The Pride of Workmanship

Andrew (Andy) Allen

Effective business leaders know the secret to success is knowing the importance of relationships as well as achievements of goals. There is no greater pride than in the team coming together to put an astronaut in space. While the astronaut is often the face of the mission, teamwork is the reason for success. The secret lies in the power of team and the combination of aptitude and attitude, as well as personal dedication. The passion, talent and commitment of each team member has made all the difference for us at the Kennedy Space Center.

This Refractive Thinker® series mirrors the importance of teamwork with a group of dedicated doctoral scholars coming together to share their research. Refractive thinkers are dedicated to connecting with business owners so that we all benefit in moving our disciplines forward, asking not only *why*, but *why not* and *what if*. Thinking is not just in or out of the box. Refractive thinkers think *beyond* the box as scholars who understand the power of creating vision and bringing that vision to successful completion through the strategies of effective project management—the focus of this volume. Project management is about the details in partnership with the team to accomplish amazing things.

Join us to learn more about the latest doctoral research behind the importance of project management in this next edition of this award winning series. Partner with these doctoral scholars regarding the importance of people and collaboration in the power of team and the pride of workmanship. Learn to see the world through their eyes, to see the power of possibilities. As our new class of 13 astronauts graduate and look to the future of returning to the moon and Mars, the power of project management lies in believing in the impact of what team can do.

For the scholars of *Vol XVIII Project Management: Strategies to Enhance Workflow and Productivity*, their missions are many. Topics in this volume include information technology security, successful project management strategies in health care, using purposeful knowledge management to save money and time, care coordination models, the impact of educational curriculum design, and new and emerging trends in project management.

People are the foundation of any organization. Celebrate their success and be grateful for their continued support. Whether planning a trip to space or completing the next big project at your company, talent and dedication of the team is what we each bring to the mission. Never forget the power of human spirit and ingenuity.

Andy Allen
NASA Astronaut
General Manager, Kennedy Space Center

About the Author....

Andrew (Andy) Allen has had a distinguished and heralded career that spans more than 40 years in the aerospace industry.

He has literally "spanned the globe" as a United States Marine Corps Lieutenant Colonel to Marine Top Gun fighter pilot to three stints as a Space Shuttle Pilot and Mission Commander before assuming more terrestrial duties.

Following his service with NASA, Andy held senior leadership positions at NASA's Kennedy Space Center, Johnson Space Center, and Headquarters in Washington, DC, where he led organizations exceeding 4,500 personnel.

He is currently serving dual roles as General Manager on the Test and Operations Support (TOSC) Contract at Kennedy Space Center and Chief Executive Officer for Aerodyne Industries LLC, which is headquartered in Cape Canaveral, FL. As TOSC GM, Andy is leading a team of more than 2,200 supporting NASA in the development of the Space Launch System, world's most powerful rocket.

In 2017, he was recognized by the National Space Club Florida Committee with the Dr. Kurt Debus Award, Florida's most prestigious space industry honor. He has received numerous other accolades throughout his illustrious career, including the Distinguished Flying Cross, Defense Superior Service Medal, Legion of Merit, NASA Outstanding Leadership Medal, and NASA Exceptional Service Medal. Visit **aerodyneindustries.com**

Preface

Welcome to the award winning Refractive Thinker® Doctoral Anthology Series. We are thrilled to have you join us for the 18th volume in the series, *The Refractive Thinker® Vol. XVIII: Project Management: Strategies to Enhance Workflow and Productivity*. Join us as we continue to celebrate the accomplishments of doctoral scholars from around the globe.

Our mission continues to be to get research off the coffee table, out of the Ivory Tower of academia, and into the hands of people who cannot only use but benefit from the many insights and wisdom found from doctoral research results and findings. The goal is to continue to bridge the gap from the halls of academia into the halls of the business world. *The Refractive Thinker®* series continues to offer a resource from the many contributing doctoral scholars as they offer their chapter summaries of doctoral research well beyond the boundaries of a traditional textbook. Instead, the goal for this series is to use refractive thinking strategies to push the boundaries beyond conventional wisdom and to explore the paths not yet traveled particularly in this evolving digital age.

As we move into the Summer of 2020, this peer-reviewed publication offers readers insights and solutions to various challenges within project management. Our hope is for you to find answers regarding these unique challenges managers and leaders face in finding effective strategies to enhance workflow and productivity. Within these pages, scholars offer insights regarding new and emerging trends in project management, successful project management strategies in health care, considerations in enterprise wide cyberthreats, preventing wastes of project costs and schedules using purposeful knowledge management, defining outsourcing and offshoring, care coordination models in accountable care organizations (ACOs), enhancing group dynamics and project success through the situational leadership lens, strategies for hiring your perfect project management, and the impact of educational curriculum design. Let these scholars help you find more effective ways forward.

This volume will continue to shape the conversation of future success in business to examine proven strategies for continued excellence and profitability that have come from the research and pens of professional academicians and scholars around the world. The premise is to think not only *outside the box*, but also *beyond the box*, to create new solutions, to ask new questions, to proceed forward on new roads not yet explored or traveled. Our premise is to review academic research in a simple to digest executive summary format to offer new ways for business leaders to think about effective practices for strategies in their business based on what new research has to offer specifically growing the future of business.

With this volume, we continue to include a section to the series where Dr. Cheryl Lentz, *The Academic Entrepreneur* concludes each chapter from a business point of view to link this doctoral research to applications for your business.

Remember, not only does *The Refractive Thinker*® series offer a physical book, we offer eBooks (Kindle, Nook, and Adobe eReader), and eChapters (individual chapters by author) that highlight the writings of your favorite Refractive Thinker® scholars, available through our website: http://www.RefractiveThinker.com, as well as www.Amazon.com . Be sure to also visit our social media to include our Facebook page, Twitter, our

YouTube Channel, and our profile and groups on LinkedIn® for further discussions regarding the many ideas presented here.

We look forward to your continued support and interest of the more than 180 scholars within *the Refractive Thinker®* doctoral community who contributed to this multi award winning anthology series from around the globe. Our mission that began with Volume 1 many years ago is to bring research out of academia for application in the world of business to provide answers to the many questions asked.

Acknowledgments

The foundation of scholarly research embraces the art of asking questions—to validate and affirm, what we do, and why. Through asking the right questions, the right answers are found. Leaders often challenge the status quo, to offer alternatives and new directions, to dare to try something bold and audacious, to try something that has never been tried before. This 19th publication of our beloved 21-time award winning *Refractive Thinker*® series required the continued belief in this new publishing model, of a peer-reviewed doctoral anthology, by those willing to continue forward on this voyage.

We are grateful for the help of many who made this collaboration possible. First, let me offer a special thank you to our **Peer Review Board**, to include Dr. Judy Blando, Dr. Ron Jones, and myself; and our **Board of Advisors** to include Brian Jud and Dr. Jody Sandwisch; and media consultant / partner, Rebecca Hall-Gruyter and her amazing team.

My gratitude extends with a well-deserved thank you to our production team: Gary Rosenberg (production specialist) and Joey Root, designer of the original Refractive Thinker® logo.

Thank you. We appreciate everyone's contributions to this scholarly collaboration.

Job well done!

My best to our continued success!

Dr. Cheryl Lentz
Managing Editor and Chief Refractive Thinker®

CHAPTER 1

New and Emerging Tools and Trends in Project Management

Dr. James Wright, Dr. Wendy Herrburger, Dr. Karen Balcanoff & Dr. Judie Brill

Traditional project management tools, as defined by the Project Management Institute (PMI), include work breakdown structures, feasibility studies, stakeholder matrices, Gantt charts, portfolio dashboards, resource management, network diagramming, performance management, risk registers, and use a suite of standard project management software (i.e., Microsoft Project) to manage projects (Barbero & Stira. 2013; Project Management Institute [PMI], 2020; Xuan, Moslehpour, & Tien, 2019). These project management tools assist the project manager (PM) in managing the definition, scope, change, planning, management, monitoring, and success of project phases, and provide relevant project data utilized in measuring project success (PMI, 2020). By taking a refractive thinking approach, project management teams seek to find new and emerging tools and trends to deliver projects.

Technology advancements in project management tools, especially in the software development arena, provide significant benefits to users and customers in project planning and execution, despite the substantial financial investment required to implement the new tools (Pellerin, Perrier, Guillot, & Leger, 2013). A study regarding useful tools and techniques with potential for enhancing project management performance, indicated the tools and techniques associated with planning, knowledge, scope, time, risk, communication, and integration had a positive impact on performance (Fernandes, Ward, & Araujo, 2013).

Advanced software management tools such as Jira, Version One, Assembla, Taigia, and Asana, address communication and integration challenges associated with large-scale projects managed by large organizations (Manole & Avramescu, 2017). These advanced software management tools, based on people management, subtask planning, and assignment of sub-tasks to people, rely on managing and empowering the teammates to take ownership and completion of the assigned tasks (Manole & Avramescu, 2017). Synchronizing project performance data from advanced tools such as Jira or Version One, with traditional project management tools (e.g., scheduling and timekeeping systems) provides the PM with real time information that can be used to analyze planned work versus actual work and provide metric data for trend analysis (Manole & Avramescu, 2017).

These advanced suites of software management tools, categorized as Agile software tools, continue to trend positively in industry, particularly for small, co-located teams developing home-grown software (Hobbs & Petit, 2017). Project development by larger organizations pose new challenges in defining the parameters associated with implementing and executing the Agile tools. These large-scale development projects, particularly those requiring high levels of integration and communication, such as Agile Scrum development, have driven development of the tools (Barbero & Stira, 2013). These large-scale projects, implemented by large organizations, changes the role of the PM from managing the daily planning and execution of project activities to a PM role in which he or she focuses on strategic initiatives, managing the stakeholders, or eliminating the role completely (Hobbs & Petit, 2017).

An Internet search of commercial project management tools revealed numerous recommendations for use in successfully managing a project. These project management tools include cloud-based tool solutions for work execution. The cloud-based tools assist in managing digital workplace environments, particularly finance, sales, human resources (HR), marketing, engineering, and legal aspects of a business that are not necessarily project management tools.

Project Management Teams

The waterfall approach to project management ensures that each segment of a project falls into the next segment without reiteration. This approach requires emphasis on the project management team interaction, more importantly than documentation (Novac & Ciochină, 2018). The collaboration of team members becomes primary to the project flow and continuation. The importance of building a team that can exist through the project and collaborate efficiently to ensure the project moves forward without repetition of steps or events is vital to team success (Novac & Ciochină, 2018). The scrum method that occurs during the waterfall approach is the direct communication and negotiation between team members on project issues and reduces the risk of disruption or process repetition (Novac & Ciochină, 2018).

The Agile manifesto calls for building projects around motivated people and supporting their needs while trusting them to produce results (Gablas, Ruzicky, & Ondrouchova, 2018). The emphasis is on their ability to communicate and collaborate with each other and the customer (Gablas et al., 2018). Building a cohesive team means identifying the role of the team members. Team members are a project resource by making decisions, budgeting, communicating information, and completing execution tasks (Abyad, 2019). Project failures are the result of poor team communication or misunderstanding problems (Abyad, 2019). Building the right team and ensuring they have complete information provides the foundation for project success.

Communication between team members is more important than documentation (Gablas et al., 2018). The responsibility for meeting project priorities rests with the project management leadership. The project management leadership needs to ensure all members understand the project goals and issues that arise during the project (Aubé, Rousseau, Brunelle, & Marques, 2018). Each member must exhibit a proactive behavior that leads to an aggressive approach to problem solving and issue resolution (Aubé et al., 2018).

Team Logistics

Team logistics can vary with extremes and can include older or younger employees, they could be collocated or spread throughout the world. Use of the waterfall approach by the team requires communication and the interaction space needs to be supportive (Yunus & Ernawati, 2018). A collocated team requires decisions about the office layout.

The open office concept will appeal to younger workers who value interaction while older workers will find it distracting (Yunus & Ernawati, 2018). Team communication outweighs the need for privacy and the importance for documentation (Novac & Ciochină, 2018). The open office concept provides opportunity for interaction and communication needed for knowledge creation (Yunus & Ernawati, 2018). The open office concept can be more inclusive. The open concept with a human centered approach provides separate zones to accommodate breaks, collaboration, and private concentration (Candido, Chakraborty, & Tjondronegoro, 2019).

Global teams provide the ability to combine specialties of a globally diverse team, provide familiarity of local needs, and be inclusive of cultural diversity (Mockaitis, Zander, & De Cieri, 2018). Connecting these teams through information communication technology requires acceptance of new strategies and financial cost. The number of employees with flexible working conditions increased between 2012 and 2017 and video conferencing will replace email as the preferred communication tool (Lye-Ching, 2017). Team meetings through electronic worker interface versus live meetings may change management strategies (Guerin, 2017). The availability of electronic worker interfacing has increased, lowering the cost for small and medium companies (Guerin, 2017).

Company leaders need to make changes to remain competitive. The growth of video conferencing is in response to the growth in workers with flexible work conditions (Lye-Ching, 2017). Company leaders have options and require changes to accommodate the workforce. The current workforce in a collocated situation requires consideration of office layout. The workers with flexible work conditions continue to drive the need for electronic interfacing. Project management teams and company employees have expectations. Employers will need to establish new office layouts and communication technology to attract and retain the best employees (Lye-Ching, 2017).

Artificial Intelligence

The age of technology took business ventures to a new level. The next generation of technology includes artificial intelligence (AI). AI is "a system's ability to correctly interpret data, to learn from such data, and to use those learnings to achieve specific goals and tasks through flexible adaption" (Kaplan & Haenlein, 2019, p. 15). The automotive industry created robotics for assembling cars; Siri and Alexa are replacing personal assistants (Williams, 2019). Despite advancement in AI, including pattern recognition and language translation, a survey of over 3,000 Chief Information Officers indicated only 37% of companies implemented AI in some form (Gartner, 2019; Tambe, Cappelli, & Yakubovich, 2019).

Artificial Intelligence in Project Management

Project management contributes to the success of an organization, but project failures gain the most attention (Allen, Alleyne, Farmer, McRae, & Turner, 2014). Relevant tasks in project management are determining, controlling, and managing complexity in a project (Castejon-Limas, Ordieres-Mere, Gonzalez-Marcos, & Gonzalez-Castro, 2011). Project management is a collective work combining the tenants of art and science (Austin, Browne, Haas, Kenyatta, & Zuluetta, 2013) and is a tool for companies to meet their project goals (Martinez & Fernandez-Rodriguez, 2017). Project managers measure cost and schedule performance to ensure customer satisfaction and project success (Nwagbogwu, 2011). Project managers are concerned whether their project will be successful including being on time and on budget, and implement controls and monitoring tools (Martinez & Fernandez-Rodriguez, 2017). To ensure project success, managers must continuously monitor the progress and use conventional methods to control the project (Ko & Cheng, 2007). These methods include neural networks, Fuzzy Cognitive Maps, and Bayesian Model (Marcelino-Sadaba, Perez-Ezcurdia, Lazcano, & Villanueva, 2013). Companies larger than 500 employees have the resources to maintain a project management department. Small businesses have limited resources and may not run projects using the recognized standards for project management (Marcelino-Sadaba et al., 2013). Small businesses often overlook the initial and final phases of a project because there are no dedicated PMs, they are inexperienced, or lack time. Companies benefit from having advanced AI project management tools to monitor progress throughout the stages of a project (Marcelino-Sadaba et al., 2013).

Artificial intelligence is programming a computer to imitate the human brain (Ko & Cheng, 2007). "Leadership is about people and AI is about machines" (Kaushik, 2018, para. 3). The McKinsey Global Institute's (2017) report *Jobs Lost, Jobs Gained: Workforce Transitions in Time of Automation* indicated by 2030, automation and AI could eliminate 75 million jobs in the United States.

From a manager's perspective, automation and AI will increase revenue and productivity, ensure accurate and immediate status of projects, and most importantly, prevent critical errors (Kaushik, 2018). The workers are concerned about unfavorable changes made to their jobs or whether companies will eliminate positions (Kaushik, 2018).

Kaushik (2018) interviewed 32 managers or technical leaders. Questions included "What percent of your cost target is expected to be reduced through AI"; "Explain the timeline of events from project initiation to closure"; [and] "If AI reduced the need for staff, what are your change management strategies?" (Kaushik, 2018, p. 24). The survey results from 26 companies, with a total of 164 automated projects, might help developers improve AI for project management. The managers indicated 68% of AI projects failed or did not meet goals (Kaushik, 2018). Other results were 92% would choose AI to reduce operating costs, 6% wanted to try new technologies, and 2% wanted to automate routine, repetitive tasks (Kaushik, 2018).

Companies must carefully evaluate employees, their skills, and their potential for staying with the company or transitioning into another position (Kaushik, 2018). One survey participant described their company of 183 employees and a new AI project would eliminate 130 people (Kaushik, 2018). There was no threat of high-performing employees losing their jobs, but they left the company because they feared being asked to leave (Kaushik, 2018). When the AI project was complete, the company did not meet their goals and reverted to the original process. The company had released employees, lost high-performing employees, the remaining employees lost trust and loyalty, and the company suffered (Kaushik, 2018).

Talent Acquisition

Artificial intelligence affects the acquisition of talented employees who can use AI in project management. Artificial intelligence improves job performance and increases e-recruitment processes (Galarza, 2017; Rodney, Valaskova, & Durana., 2019). With online applications, an average of 250 apply for any given position (Polli, 2019). Prior to AI, recruiters manually reviewed resumes, which was time consuming and led to unconscious biases (Polli, 2019). Recruiters limited their application review to those, in their opinion, who were the best fit (Polli, 2019). Artificial intelligence makes the recruitment process cost effective (Bongard, 2019). Bongard (2019) surveyed 2,400 businesspeople where AI was most useful. The results indicated 1,632 individuals used AI to source candidates and 1,368 individuals used AI to screen candidates (Bongard, 2019).

The quality of data relates to the effective use of AI (Smith, 2019). Humans teach AI by applying algorithms (Polli, 2019). The characteristics of previously successful applicants are programmed into the algorithms used to review new applicants (Polli, 2019). If the previous employees were White men, the algorithm will produce biases to White men (Polli, 2019). Programming technicians' bias adds to the difficulty of hiring a diverse workforce (Galarza, 2017). The good news is biasness is removed if AI is redesigned (Bongard, 2019).

Employee Retention

Because of the possibility of high-performing employees leaving a company implementing AI, management needs to make better decisions about salaries and market demand for skills (Moore & Bokelberg, 2019). This helps companies retain employees. Employees have difficulty maintaining skillsets to keep up with the fast-paced advancement of technology (Moore & Bokelberg, 2019). IBM developed AI to predict skill requirements and compare the requirements with current employees' skills (Moore & Bokelberg, 2019). Bongard's (2019) research indicated 73% of the business people's responses were AI benefits the company and saved time, and 49% believed AI removed human bias. As skillsets begin to change, IBM can target new hires with needed skillsets (Moore & Bokelberg, 2019). IBM's HR department used AI to improve the employee's experience and improve business outcomes. Time to hire decreased 50% and employee engagement increased 20% (Moore & Bokelberg, 2019). Wilkinson, Podhorska, and Siekelova (2019) surveyed 3,600 business people to determine the reason leaders are adopting AI. Of the responses, 82% believed AI would allow their organization to sustain a competitive advantage; 77% believed it would allow their organization to move into new business; and 72% believed new companies using AI would enter the market (Williams, 2019). Artificial intelligence contributes to process success and is a benefit when implementing the new and emerging trends in progress delivery. Project management software is complex, allowing PMs to rely on computer results instead of the meticulous *pen and paper* calculations. Once programmed, computers will ensure accurate and current data. Advanced AI will increase revenue, improve productivity, and save time; however, employees are concerned that the use of AI will reduce or eliminate their roles in companies.

Waterfall, Agile, and Hybrid Delivery Method

As project management methods and tools progress, the emergence of Agile and hybrid delivery methods is of interest to organizations (Campanelli & Parreiras, 2015). A hybrid approach uses traditional waterfall methods with Agile aspects to deliver projects that improve delivery time and quality (Noll & Beecham, 2019). Straight Agile project methods focus on business alignment, customer involvement and collaboration, increase in quality and productivity (Noll & Beecham, 2019) Traditional waterfall methods are the tried and true method of project delivery (Noll & Beecham, 2019). Agile and hybrid deliveries are increasing and are the new way to deliver project (Campanelli & Parreiras, 2015).

Traditional Waterfall Project Delivery Methods

A traditional waterfall project methodology tracks milestone throughout the project (Nambiar, Maurya, Ramesh, & Arora, 2019). Organizations use waterfall methodologies because of the ease of collecting large amounts of data on successful project delivery, quality, and team satisfaction (Ciancarini, Mazzara, Messina, Sillitti, & Succi, 2020). Conflicting indicators exist with new emerging project delivery types, the use of any method does not have a high correlation to project success (Pace, 2019).

Traditional waterfall delivery relies on a step-by-step approach with dependent relationships defined (Adiga, 2019). As projects progress with the waterfall delivery method, risks are calculated as each dependent activity is affected (Nambiar et al., 2019). The waterfall approach allows PMs to take immediate action on issues since a clear critical path is visible with the project scheduling tools at their disposal (Barbero & Stira, 2013). Additional drawbacks to the traditional waterfall approach are the strict rigidness of the method and no going back mentality, and difficulty in adjusting the scope (Barbero & Stira, 2013). Clients are pressuring for quicker project delivery, which led to the emergence of the Agile delivery method (Ciancarini et al., 2020).

Agile Delivery Method

Agile projects emerged with software implementations in mind (Doležel, 2018). Since the introduction to the broader project management community, Agile expanded into other project management forums (Marinho, Noll, Richardson, & Beecham, 2019). Marinho et al. (2019) found that software development and team locations are no longer the binding factors traditionally held by Agile projects. Noll and Beecham (2019) found that projects using a hybrid will not adhere to the strict principles that Agile projects uphold.

Agile projects use a sprint-based or iteration approach that tracks projects in small pre-defined units (Poe & Seeman, 2019). When completed, measuring progress against these smaller units are viewed as a project success (Poe & Seeman, 2019). Teams use Agile with the vision of faster delivery and increased quality; however, the vision not always the realized. Strictly adhering to the principles of Agile is critical for teams to determine which delivery method is best for the specific project (Poe & Seeman, 2019).

A traditional waterfall team structure can contain larger groups of specialists and team members. An Agile or hybrid team structure is smaller with members who have a targeted skillset, are self-managed and feel a great sense of empowerment. Agile teams are led by a Scrum Master who guides the team and removes any obstacles in their way to deliver a project (Pereira, 2019). The benefits of Agile are the ability to immediately respond to change, and increased customer collaboration. According to Pereira, the six factors that contribute to Agile projects are daily stand up meetings, team cohesiveness, weekly planning, sprint review, script planning, and iterative development. These factors contribute to the success of a project delivered by the Agile delivery method (Pereira, 2019).

Hybrid Project Delivery Method

Hybrid project delivery methods evolved because project teams and companies used customized processes combined with a traditional waterfall method and aspects of Agile (Paolo et al., 2019). Individualized hybrid methods vary within companies with common characteristics of a traditional waterfall and Agile delivery processes (Paolo et al., 2019). Companies choose these methods out of necessity (Akhmetshin et al., 2019). Leaders have seen limited successes with only Agile or waterfall delivery approaches and as a result, have turned to an individualized method (Ariza, Mozo, & Quintero, 2018).

According to Noll and Beecham (2019), benefits of using a hybrid delivery approach are the effects they can have on an organization and the organizational change process. By introducing the hybrid approach, companies use portions of their known current processes throughout the organization and introduce new concepts without committing to large-scale changes. Easing into this type of change management has been successful in organizations (Jabar, Ali, Jusoh, Abdullah, & Mohanarajah, 2019). This contributes to the appeal and success of using a hybrid delivery approach.

Conclusion

In line with a refractive thinker frame of mind, based on research and interpenetration of existing information, challenges exist for PMs in using new and emerging tools and trends. With global teams prevalent in organizations, it is important to embrace new tools and trends to ensure project success. Team locations continue to be a concern in the global markets with conflicting time zones, employee's availability to connect, and to ensure clear understanding of project goals (Mockaitis et al., 2018).

The emergence of AI and data analytics will reduce reliance on employees for tasks regarding data mining and project tools to make project reporting easier without the constant manual intervention that is the current standard. Artificial intelligence and data mining are the fastest growing areas in project management and the area of the greatest interest to teams. Shifting focus from manual interventions allows employees more time to work on project deliverables and work through project issues and problems.

Project delivery methodologies such as Agile and hybrid are a company's preference with no clear preferred method emerging as one that guarantees project success. Different aspects of delivery methods are appealing within organizations. Each organizational leader chooses the method that best fits his or her company's culture. Project management leaders need to start projects with a solid foundation to increase the opportunity for success. The project management team needs to ensure all areas of expertise are represented. These members need to communicate with the team and customer. Productive communication between team members eliminates repetition of action and moves the project forward. Leaders need to utilize multiple management strategies that accommodate collocated and global project management teams. Management is challenged to build a team that understands project priorities and are capable of communication face-to-face or through electronic worker interface.

THOUGHTS FROM THE ACADEMIC ENTREPRENEUR

The Problem to be Solved:
- What new tools are emerging in the project management community to assist project managers in successfully executing their projects?

The Goals:
- To define the emerging project management tools and trends in the 21st century timeframe that can be applied by project managers.
- To understand the effect of emerging technologies on project delivery and how artificial intelligence effects project management, talent acquisition, and employee retention.
- To build proactive project management teams and provide resources to enable them to be refractive thinkers.

The Questions to Ask:
- Are the emerging project management tools and trends applicable to all types of projects, or are they limited in the applicability (i.e., software development projects)?
- Are project management leaders placing enough emphasis on building the best project management team?
- Are there benefits having advanced artificial intelligence project management tools to monitor project progress?
- How does management address employee layoffs when artificial intelligence is implemented?

Today's Business Application:
- The emerging tools and trends in project management (e.g., Version One, Agile) can provide deeper project performance insight based on the specific resources and tasks which can

help the project manager re-direct resources and priorities to meet project objectives.

- Provide project management leaders items of consideration for project management team assembly and facilitating communication between team members.
- The use of emerging technologies will increase revenue and productivity, ensure accurate and immediate status of projects, and prevent critical errors.
- Management needs to understand emerging technologies can replace employee jobs.

REFERENCES

Abyad, A. (2019). Project management: Science or a craft? *Middle East Journal of Business, 14*(1), 4–16. https://dx.doi.org/10.5742/MEJB.2019.93608

Adiga, S. K. (2019). Challenges faced by managers while migrating from waterfall to Agile methodology in service-based IT companies in India. *Master's Thesis, Dublin Business School*. Retrieved from https://esource.dbs.ie/handle/10788/3648

Akhmetshin, E. M, Romanov, P. Y., Zakieva, R. R., Zhminko, A. E., Aleshko, R. A., & Makarov, A. L. (2019). Modern approaches to innovative project management in entrepreneurship education: A review of methods and applications in education. *Journal of Entrepreneurship Education, 22*(1S), 1-15. Retrieved from https://www.abacademies.org

Allen, M., Alleyne, D., Farmer, C., McRae, A., & Turner, C. (2014). A framework for project success. *Journal of IT and Economic Development, 5*(2), 1-17. Retrieved from hhtp://www.tandfonline.com

Ariza, H. M., Mozo, V. R., & Quintero, H. M., (2018). Methodology for the Agile development of software based on a guide for the body of knowledge of scrum (SBOKTM Guide). *International Journal of Applied Engineering Research, 13*, 11479-11483. Retrieved from https://www.ripublication.com/ijaer18/ijaerv13n14_17.pdf

Aubé, C., Rousseau, V., Brunelle, E., & Marques, D. (2018). The relevance of being "on the same page" to succeed as a project team: A moderated mediation model. *Motivation & Emotion, 42*, 804–815. https://dx.doi.org/10.1007/s11031-018-9706-2

Austin, C., Browne, W., Haas, B. Kenyatta, E., & Zuluetta, S. (2013). Application of project management in higher education. *Journal of Economic Development, Management, IT, Finance and Marketing, 5(2)*, 75-99. Retrieved from http://www.gsmi-ijgb.com

Barbero, M. C., & Stira, C. (2013). How emerging tools can support traditional project management tools: A real case. Paper presented at PMI® Global Congress 2013—North America, New Orleans, LA. Newtown Square, PA: Project Management Institute. Retrieved from https://www.pmi.org

Bongard, A. (2019). Automating talent acquisition: Smart recruitment, predictive hiring algorithms, and the data-driven nature of artificial intelligence. *Psychological Issues in Human Resource Management, 7*(1), 36-41. Retrieved from https://addletonacademicpublishers.com

Campanelli, A. S., & Parreiras, F. S. (2015). Agile methods tailoring–A systematic literature review. *Journal of Systems and Software, 110*, 85-100. https://dx.doi.org/10.1016/j.jss.2015.08.035

Candido, C., Chakraborty, P., & Tjondronegoro, D. (2019). The rise of office design in high-performance, open-plan environments. *Buildings, 9*(4), 100-116. https://dx.doi.org/10.3390/buildings9040100

Castejon-Limas, M., Ordieres-Mere, J., Gonzalez-Marcos, A., & Gonzalez-Castro, V. (2011). Effort estimates through project complexity. *Annals of Operations Research, 186*, 395-406. https://dx.doi.org/10.1007/s10479-010-0776-0

Ciancarini, P., Mazzara, M., Messina, A., Sillitti, A. & Succi, G. (2020). Proceedings of 6th International Conference in Software Engineering for Defense Applications. https://dx.doi.org/10.1007/978-3-030-14687-0

Doležel, M. (2018). Possibilities of applying institutional theory in the study of hybrid software development concepts and practices. In M. Kuhrmann (Eds.), *PROFES 2018*. LNCS, *11271*, 441–448. Springer. https://dx.doi.org/10.1007/978-3-030-03673-7

Fernandes, G., Ward, S., & Araujo, M. (2013). Identifying useful project management practices: A mixed methodology approach. *International Journal of Information Systems and Project Management, 1*(4), 5-21. https://dx.doi.org/10.12821/ijispm010401

Gablas, B., Ruzicky, E., & Ondrouchova, M. (2018). The change in management style during the course of a project from the classical to the agile approach. *Journal of Competitiveness, 4*, 38-53. https://dx.doi.org/10.7441/joc.2018.04.03

Galarza, M. (2017). The changing nature of accounting. *Strategic Finance*, 50-54. Retrieved from https://sfmagazine.com

Gartner. (2019). Gartner survey shows 37 percent of organizations have implemented AI in some form. Retrieved from http://www.Gartner.com

Hobbs, B., & Petit, Y. (2017). Agile approaches on large projects in large organizations. *Project Management Journal, 48*(3), 3-19. https://dx.doi.org/10.1177/875697281704800301

Jabar, M. A., Ali, N. M., Jusoh, Y. Y., Abdullah, S., & Mohanarajah, S., (2019). Adaptive and dynamic hybrid model for software project management: A review on its clarity and usage to improve project success. *Applied Mechanics and Materials, 892*, 38–45. https://dx.doi.org/10.4028/www.scientific.net/amm.892.38-45

Kaplan, A., & Haenlein, M. (2019). Siri, Siri, in my hand: Who's the fairest in the land? On the interpretations, illustrations, and implications of artificial intelligence. *Business Horizons, 62*(1), 15-25. https://dx.doi.org/10.1016/j.bushor.2018.08.004

Kaushik, S. (2018). Critical parameters for successful process automation. *Software Quality Professional, 20*(4), 22-32. Retrieved from https://asq.org

Ko, C. H., & Cheng, M. Y. (2007). Dynamic prediction of project success using artificial intelligence. *Journal of Construction Engineering and Management, 133*, 316-320. https://dx.doi.org/10.1061/(ASCE)0733-9364(2007)133:4(316)

Lye-Ching, L. (2017). Video conferencing to build business relationships. *Computerworld Hong Kong, 62*. Retrieved from http://www.cw.com.hk

Manole, M., & Avramescu, M. (2017). A comparative analysis of agile project management tools. *Economy Informatics, 17*(1), 25-31. Retrieved from http://www.economyinformatics.ase.ro

Marcelino-Sadaba, S., Perez-Ezcurdia, A., Lazcano, A. M. E., & Villanueva, P. (2013). Project risk management methodology for small firms. *International Journal of Project Management*, 32, 327-340. https://dx.doi.org/10.1016/j.jproman.2013.05.009

Marinho, M., Noll, J., Richardson, I., & Beecham, S. (2019). Plan-driven approaches are alive and kicking in agile global software development. *International Symposium on Empirical Software Engineering and Measurement* Retrieved from https://arxiv.org/pdf/1906.08895.pdf

Martinez, D. M., & Fernandez-Rodriguez, J. C. (2017). Artificial intelligence applied to project success: A literature review. *International Journal of Artificial Intelligence and Interactive Multimedia*, 3(5), 77-82. https://dx.doi-org/10.9781/ijimai.2015.3510

McKinsey Global Institute. (2017). Jobs lost; jobs gained: Workforce transitions in a time of automation. Retrieved from https://www.mckinsey.com

Moore, T., & Bokelberg, E. (2019). How IBM incorporates artificial intelligence into strategic workforce planning. *People + Strategy*, 42(4), 52-55. Retrieved from http://store.hrps.org

Mockaitis, A. I., Zander, L., & De Cieri, H. (2018). The benefits of global teams for international organizations: HR implications. *International Journal of Human Resource Management*, 29, 2137–2158. https://dx.doi.org/10.1080/09585192.2018.1428722

Nambiar, K. D., Maurya, R. S., Ramesh, A. P., & Arora M. (2019). Application of waterfall design process in designing of a holistic system for children with hearing impairment in resource-constrained settings. In A. Chakrabarti (Eds), *Research into design for a connected world: Smart innovation, systems, and technologies, 134*, 929-940. https://dx.doi.org/10.1007/978-981-13-5974-3_80

Noll, J., & Beecham S. (2019) How agile is hybrid agile?: An analysis of the HELENA Data. In X. Franch T. Männistö& S. Martínez-Fernández S. (Eds.), *Product-focused software process improvement. PROFES 2019. Lecture Notes in Computer Science*, 11915. Springer, Cham. https://dx.doi.org/10.1007/978-3-030-35333-9_25

Novac, C., & Ciochină, R.-S. (2018). Challenges of applying agile principles and values to IT project management. *Journal of Entrepreneurship, Management & Innovation*, 14(4), 43–62. https://dx.doi.org/10.7341/20181442

Nwagbogwu, D. C. (2011). *The correlation between project management effectiveness and project success* (Doctoral dissertation). Available from ProQuest Dissertations and Theses database. (UMI No. 3434599)

Pace, M. (2019) A correlational study on project management methodology and project success. *Journal of Engineering, Project and Production Management*, 9(2), 56-65. https://dx.doi.org/10.2478/jeppm-2019-0007

Paolo, T., Klunder, J., Kupper, S., Raffo, D., MacDonell, S. G., Munch, J., Pfahl, D., Linssen, O. & Kuhrmann, M. (2019). What are hybrid development methods made of?: An evidence-based characterization. In *Proceedings of the international* conference on software processes (ICSSP'19). IEEE Press, 105-114. https://dx.doi.org/10.1109/ICSSP.2019.00022

Pellerin, R., Perrier, N., Guillot, X., & Leger, P. (2013). Project characteristics, project management software utilization and project performance: An impact analysis based on real project data. *International Journal of Information Systems and Project Management, 1*(3), 5-26. https://dx.doi.org/10.12821/ijispm010301

Pereira, T. P. (2019). Scrum and XP Agile practices used by project managers contribution toward software project success. Masters Thesis. *Dublin Business School.* Retrieved from https://esource.dbs.ie.handle/10788/3925

Poe. L. F., & Seeman, E. (2019). An empirical study of post-production software code quality when employing the Agile rapid delivery methodology. *Proceedings of the Conference on Information Systems Applied Research.* Retrieved from http://proc.conisar.org

Polli, F. (2019). Using AI to eliminate bias from hiring. *Harvard Business Review Digital Articles*, 2-4. Retrieved from https://hbr.org/

Project Management Institute (PMI). (2019). *Developing a project management toolbox.* Retrieved from https://www.pmi.org/

Rodney, H., Valaskova, K., & Durana, P. (2019). The artificial intelligence recruitment process: How technological advancements have reshaped job application and selection practices. *Psychological Issues in Human Resource Management, 7*(1), 42-47. Retrieved from https://addletonacademicpublishers.com/

Smith, D. (2019). AI in data governance. *Strategic Finance*, 60-61. Retrieved from https://sfmagazine.com

Tambe, P., Cappelli, P., & Yakubovich, V. (2019). Artificial intelligence in human resources management: Challenges and a path forward. *California Management Review, 61*(4), 15-42. https://dx.doi.org/10.1177/0008125619867910

Wilkinson, W., Podhorska, I., & Siekelova, A. (2019). Does the growth of artificial intelligence and automation shape talent attraction and retention? *Psychological Issues in Human Resource Management, 7*(1), 30-35. Retrieved from https://addletonacademicpublishers.com/

Williams, R. (2019). Artificial intelligence assistants in the library: Siri, Alexa, and beyond. *Online Searcher, 43*(3), 10-14. Retrieved from http://www.infotoday.com/onlinesearcher/

Yunus, E. N., & Ernawati, E. (2018). Productivity paradox?: The impact of office redesign on employee productivity. *International Journal of Productivity and Performance Management,* 67, 1918–1939. https://dx.doi.org/10.1108/IJPPM-12-2017-0350

Xuan, Q. L. H., Moslehpour, M., & Tien, D. T. (2019). An evaluation of project management tools and techniques in Vietnam. *Management Science Letters, 9*(2), 283-300. https://dx.doi.org/10.5267/j.msl.2018.11.011

About the Authors...

Dr. James Wright resides in Perrysburg Ohio. Dr Jim holds three accredited degrees; a Bachelor of Science (BS) in Human Resources Management from Park University; A Master of Arts in Organizational Management (MAOM) from University of Phoenix; and a Doctor of Business Administration (DBA) in Leadership from Walden University.

Dr. Jim is a Senior Clinical Specialist working in Behavioral Health, and a Retired U.S. Navy Senior Chief. Additional published work includes his dissertation: *Manufacturing Managers' Leadership Efficacy in the Context of Reduced Union Influence* and *Nonprofit and For-Profit Health care Organization Satisfaction based on Compensation Packages* in The Refractive Thinker® Vol XIV

To reach Dr. James Wright for information on business or leadership consulting, please **e-mail: jwright2962@gmail.com**

Dr. Wendy J. Mizerek-Herrburger resides in the Space coast town of Cocoa Beach, Florida. Dr. Wendy holds several accredited degrees; a Bachelor of Science (BS) in Marketing from the University of Florida; a Master of Science in Industrial Engineering (MSIE) from University of Central Florida; and a Doctor of Business Administration (DBA) from Walden University.

Dr. Wendy is the Director of Business Operations at Jacobs Technology, with the Test, Operations Support Contract at the Kennedy Space Center, FL. She holds a current Project Management Institute (PMI) certification in Project Management.

Dr. Wendy co-authored "Nonprofit and For-Profit Health care Organization Satisfaction based on Compensation Packages" in *The Refractive Thinker® Vol XIV* and "Doctoral Mentoring and Research Leading to Emerging Technologies" in *The Refractive Thinker® Vol IX*. She has also co-authored published articles *Engaging Employees Successful in Project Management Practices* and *Best Practices in Doctoral Retention: Mentoring*. Dr. Wendy gained professional and academic expertise with doctoral study, *A Project Management Perspective of the Glass Cliff Phenomenon*.

To reach Dr. Wendy J. Mizerek-Herrburger for information on guest speaking, consulting, or doctoral coaching, please **e-mail: drwendyherrburger@outlook.com**

Dr. Karen Balcanoff resides in Jacksonville, Florida. Dr. Karen is Director of the Bachelor in Organizational Management program at St. Johns River State College with campuses in Palatka, St. Augustine, and Orange Park, Florida. Dr. Karen began the bachelor program in January 2011 and teaches, advises, and mentors all students in the program. Dr. Karen received her Bachelors of Science in Health Administration (BHA) from the University of North Florida, Master of Business Administration (MBA) from the University of North Florida, and her Doctorate of Business Administration (DBA) from Walden University.

Dr. Karen co-authored "Nonprofit and For-Profit Health care Organization Satisfaction based on Compensation Packages" in *The Refractive Thinker® Vol XIV* and "Doctoral Mentoring and Research Leading to Emerging Technologies" in *The Refractive Thinker® Vol IX*. She has also co-authored published articles *Engaging Employees Successful in Project Management Practices* and *Best Practices in Doctoral Retention: Mentoring*. Dr. Karen gained professional and academic expertise with her doctoral study, *The Effect of Communication on Hospital Nursing and Morale*.

To reach Dr. Karen Balcanoff for information on professional editing, or guest speaking, please **e-mail: karenbalcanoff@sjrstate.edu**

Dr. Judie L. Brill resides in the mountain town of Bailey, Colorado. Dr. Judie is a Consultant for the pharmaceutical industry specializing in business process, strategies, lean leadership, and project management. She enjoys the interaction with numerous companies, employees and regulatory agencies striving to provide a pathway to excellence within diverse organizations. She is a member of the IPSE Mountain States Chapter and other Pharmaceutical and Lean Six Sigma Organizations.

Dr. Judie is President and CEO of Brill Consulting, Inc., a Professional organizational consulting company. Her doctoral study, A *Company's Response* to *Culture Change in Time of Reorganization*, provided her the opportunity to gain professional and academic expertise to facilitate improvements in the changing world of manufacturing and pharmaceutical industries. Dr. Judie also co-authored "Nonprofit and For-Profit Health care Organization Satisfaction based on Compensation Packages" in *The Refractive Thinker® Vol XIV* and "Doctoral Mentoring and Research Leading to Emerging Technologies" in *The Refractive Thinker® Vol IX*. She has also co-authored published articles *Engaging Employees Successful in Project Management Practices* and *Best Practices in Doctoral Retention: Mentoring*.

To reach Dr. Judie L. Brill for information on professional editing or guest speaking, please **email: judie.brill@gmail.com**

CHAPTER 2

Successful Project Management Strategies at Health Care Organizations

Dr. Frank Musmar

The complex nature of the health care industry and the complex nature of projects within health care might contribute to the lack of project success. For example, Flynn and Hartfield (2016) referred to health care quality improvement initiatives as being complex from multiple active components, referring to the complex interplay among stakeholders (patients, providers, and clinical units), processes, and outcomes. Baird and Boak (2016) and Garrety, McLoughlin, Dalley, Wilson, and Ping (2016) similarly noted significant challenges associated with electronic health records (EHRs or EMRs) projects. Although Karol (2015) found that organizational factors such as leadership, culture, and corporate processes influence project success in health care, these findings are neither tangible nor concrete to benefit project managers. The health care industry continues to face challenges, such as escalating health care costs, decreasing reimbursement, changes in legislation, and other factors (Mehta & Ahmad, 2016). Through this case study, I explored how one health care organization modeled successful project management practices. In this chapter of *The Refractive Thinker®*, I presented an overview of successful project management strategies at health care organizations

Background: Importance of Implementing Successful Project Management Strategies

Projects continue to fail at a high rate regardless of the type of project, or the industry from which they originate (Ramazani & Jergeas, 2015), wasting billions of dollars each year (Harrington & Frank, 2015). Harrington and Frank (2015) found that 75% of projects failed before they ever reached implementation. Wasted resources are unproductive and can undermine business success and competitive advantage of health care organizations. Some business leaders experience poor project performance from a lack of strategies to manage projects successfully, resulting in wasted resources and a loss in profitability. The purpose of this study was to explore strategies that leaders use to manage projects successfully in health care. The success of health care organizations directly influences their ability to uphold their mission statements. Health care facilities exist to serve individuals and communities; enhancing their performance can have a cascading positive effect on society. When health care organizations are successful, the leaders of those organizations can ensure that important health and wellness services are available to those who need them. If project leaders understand project management strategies better, it may improve project success rates and decrease wasted resources. Leaders of business who can optimize their resources have the potential to increase business success.

Importance of Effective Project Management

The benefits of projects are retaining business value, and providing an opportunity to undertake the core businesses of firms, which generates business value (Valčić, Dimitrić, & Dalsaso, 2016). One basic function of projects is to serve as a component of business operations (Valčić et al., 2016). Business operations facilitate resource allocation to accomplish work, which is the function of projects (Killen & Hunt, 2013). Projects are not limited to business operations. Projects are effective to implement corporate vision and strategy (Hyväri, 2016). For example, leaders who wish to embrace environmental sustainability as one of their corporate strategies may use projects to demonstrate organizational sustainability endeavors (Sánchez & Schneider, 2014). Successful projects and project execution are relevant concepts for not just implementing but also managing corporate strategy.

Projects serve as catalysts for new strategy development to drive business success and competitive advantage that stem from partnerships that arise from projects. Meng and Boyd (2017) described these catalysts as co-creation projects that leverage the strengths of project-partner organizations to achieve a competitive advantage over others in the market. Co-creation projects promote strategy development by enhancing innovation capabilities, reducing the cost of existing innovation approach, minimizing disruption to existing operations, and promoting continuous quality improvement to increase firm's competitive position (Meng & Boyd, 2017).

Why Projects Fail

Researchers have different perspectives on why projects fail, and the literature does not offer a consensus definition of project success or project failure. In this section, I categorized the common reasons why projects fail into people issues, process issues, and project issues.

People Issues

Dwivedi et al. (2015) attributed project failure to problems related to people issues at multiple levels of project and organizational authority, causing a lack of communication within projects. For example, insufficient project sponsorship by top-level leaders, weak project personnel, and lack of end-user involvement in usability testing contribute to project failure (Dwivedi et al., 2015).

Duffield and Whitty (2015) concluded that insufficient project sponsorship indicated a lack of clear senior leader ownership and support of projects. Similarly, Flyvbjerg (2014) found that weak leadership and leaders' perceptions prevented them from applying lessons learned from other projects, contributing to higher levels of project failure. Duffield and Whitty (2015) concurred, stating that failure to learn from lessons learned is a pervasive problem, influenced substantially by the people and culture of an organization.

Hjelmbrekke, Hansen, and Lohne (2015) stated that multiple issues exist at the project team level. Lack of team integration, lack of attentiveness to policies, realistic expectations of the project, and project leaders' inability to engage stakeholders effectively were common problems (Anthopoulos, Reddick, Giannakidou, & Mavridis, 2016). Project teams suffer from wishful thinking and friction among both internal and external project participants (Dwivedi et al., 2015).

Process Issues

Process issues also contribute to project failure. Process issues related to translating the strategic goals of the organization into tangible projects (Hjelmbrekke et al., 2015). If organizational leaders are unable to outline and realize the organizational strategies, initiating appropriate projects and moving them to complete successfully would be difficult. Process issues exist throughout the projects' lifecycles. Hussain and Mkpojiogu (2016) indicated that poorly designed project selection and prioritization processes for Lean Six Sigma projects in health care are partially to blame for project failure.

A highly structured project management approach is typically associated with formal project planning activities (Khattack, Mustafa, & Shah, 2016) that span the entire project lifecycle (Anthopoulos et al., 2016). Although structured processes are necessary to maintain control, flexibility is also required. Process flexibility is important for creativity, the emergence of new ideas, and disruptive innovation that can provide organizations a chance at a competitive advantage (Zuo, Zillante, Zhao, & Xia, 2014).

Project Issues

An inverse relationship exists between project complexity and project success (Moore, Payne, Autry, & Griffis, 2016). Dao, Kermanshachi, Shane, Anderson, and Hare (2016) referred to project complexity as variables that confound, complicate, or make projects difficult to manage. Floricel, Michela, and Piperca (2016) indicated that project complexity often results in uncertainty, risk, and cost. Project teams must make continual adjustments to their project plans. Because most of these factors are multifaceted, which makes project management more complex and potentially compromises project success (Khattack et al., 2016).

Some project complexity factors are related to internal variables such as changing project type and size (Klein, 2016) and magnitude of change orders and frequency of workarounds (Kermanshachi, Dao, Shane, & Anderson, 2016). Others are more logistical, such as permitting and approvals (Dao et al., 2016) or technological challenges related to interfaces (Khattack et al., 2016). The final complexity category relates to macro environmental factors such as dynamic market conditions, geopolitical and social issues, and social and cultural systems (Klein, 2016).

Unique Characteristics of Project Management in Health Care

Implementation of health care projects could save lives, prevent injury, or have other tangible patient safety and well-being outcomes (Crema & Verbano, 2016). Health care projects also increase efficiency, enhance core business functions, and reduce unnecessary costs, which benefit patients (Skoien et al., 2016). Project Management Institute (2018) indicated that relationship management is a component of stakeholder management. Stakeholder management in health care projects is critical to project success (Oostveen, Ubbink, Mens, Pompe, & Vermeulen, 2016). Some clinician stakeholders in an EHR implementation project experienced emotional distress, feelings of personal loss, and grief in replacing their paper charts (Reed & Card, 2016).

Health care project leaders should prioritize stakeholder management. In health care, stakeholder management equates to gaining staff and clinicians' buy-in and generating professional enthusiasm for various projects (Andreassen, Kjekshus, & Tjora, 2015). Generating project enthusiasm is essential in health care to engage clinicians, reduce the necessity of governance oversight, and elevate organizational performance (Boonstra, 2017).

Health care projects are also characterized by an overemphasis on project execution because of the competing forces of stakeholder management and clinical quality excellence (Skoien et al., 2016). Although project leaders may be hesitant to implement projects full-scale because of certain stakeholders–health care providers (Oostveen et al., 2016), health care professionals also desire to move toward clinical quality improvements as quickly as possible to help other stakeholders–patients.

Best Practices in Project Management

The discipline of project management is constantly changing. However, the literature outlines project management best practices into these categories: governance, infrastructure, corporate culture, communication, and project leaders (Bresnan, 2016).

Governance

Volden and Samset (2017) defined governance as processes, systems, and regulations that ensure project success. There are multiple dimensions to governance structures. The first is governance in the context of the organizational structures of a single firm perspective in which the focus of governance is on meeting the strategic and technical needs of the firm. Joslin and Müller (2016) added that governance outlines the strategic and institutional needs of the firm, considering external environmental factors such as political, environmental, and statutory requirements. The second is governance from the project, where leaders limit their involvement to macro level issues that governance-related and not the management and control aspects. A governance framework based on project perspective should provide mechanisms to guide project success versus the top leader's micromanaging projects (Van der Hoorn & Whitty, 2017).

Joslin and Müller (2016) suggested that an appropriate governance structure should focus on processes and not on control or outcome measures. To elaborate further, Joslin and Müller advised top leaders to consider outlining practical process guidelines to help project teams achieve success. Joslin and Müller's conclusions were suggesting limiting the role of governance in developing overarching strategic mechanisms for project success, and not the control-oriented tactics.

Infrastructure

Leaders have a responsibility to create an infrastructure that ensures project success. Leaders provide these through their decision-making authority and power to allocate resources (Hermano & Martín-Cruz, 2016). Specific examples of infrastructure include coordinating activities that promote project generation, assisting with project budgeting and funding, creating project tools, preparing agreements, developing quality assurance methods, offering communication and legal advice, and in some cases offer project management certification (Chang, 2017).

Corporate Culture

Leaders play a major role in establishing organizational culture, and culture is critical to project success (Hermano & Martín-Cruz, 2016). Hutchinson-Krupat and Chao (2014) found that when the organizational culture was more accepting of failure, participants took more risk, which led to higher levels of innovation. Karol (2015) also affirmed the association of innovative culture with long-term project success. Corporate culture does not materialize from anything, but rather the cultivation of leaders. Leaders are responsible for facilitating change or actively manage their corporate culture to realize its benefits. Karol argued that an environment that encourages innovation and engenders trust is necessary. Grant (2016) also warned that culture change is difficult and takes time.

Leaders need to pay attention to the processes used to change the culture (Grant, 2016). Cultural changes which based on strategy and integrated into core operations (built-in) will create a sustainable corporate reputation (Chang, 2017). Cultural changes treated as initiatives or designed around tactics (bolted-on) are disingenuous and perhaps, at their worst, incompatible with business objectives (Chang, 2017).

Built-in cultural changes reorient the organization based on common understanding, shared purpose, and maximize stakeholder value (Chatman, 2014). Grant (2016) proposed giving employees the latitude to think innovatively, and as individuals. Giving employees autonomy and the opportunity to think innovatively promotes a balance between cohesion and dissent and undergirds a strong culture (Grant, 2016). Changes require a shift in focus from projects and programs to organizational operations (Grant, 2016).

Communication

There are no one-size-fits-all frameworks to govern how and where communication should occur (Burga & Rezania, 2017). Communication options exist depending on stakeholders' involvement, their communication preferences, the urgency of the content, and the availability of resources (Stanciu, Condrea, & Zamfir, 2016). Foss et al. (2016) argued that communication occurs in both structured and unstructured environments. Unstructured environments are conducive to communication-related to new projects or project launches, where structured spaces are relevant for project joining purposes (Foss, Frederiksen, & Rullani, 2016).

Stanciu et al. (2016) indicated that communication is the lynchpin for project success and that all constituents from the organization, but especially management, should participate. Although no panacea for project communication exists, leaders should understand the critical role communication plays in ensuring alignment (Stanciu et al., 2016). Given the availability of different types of communication methods and the flexibility of where communication can occur, leaders should consider deliberate communication strategies as part of their project strategy.

Project Leaders

The model leaders are very important in project success (Maqbool et al., 2017). Hermano and Martín-Cruz (2016) explained that top leaders' ability to influence project success translated to firm performance. This correlation existed regardless of firms' industry, size, years in business, or their orientation toward projects (Hermano & Martín-Cruz, 2016). Meng and Boyd (2017) found that among several factors, leaders' vision, values, performance, and ability to drive project spirit explained some variance in project success. leaders who role model behaviors have a positive influence on their employees, specifically for projects involving change management (Stoffers & Mordant-Dols, 2015).

Hassan, Bashir, and Abbas (2017) found that extraversion, agreeableness, and openness to experience were direct positive indicators of project success. It may be difficult to exude project spirit if leaders are not attentive to projects. A second-best practice in the area of leader characteristics is leader attention. Hessler (2016) found that in some industries, top leaders largely ignore the project management capabilities of teams working on smaller-scale projects. Maqbool et al. (2017) linked leader qualities with higher levels of project success and posited that proactive leaders have better project success rates. Samset and Volden (2016) argued that these assessments help leaders forecast the potential for project success. If leaders determine that projects have lower probabilities of success, they can discontinue those projects and minimize sunk costs (Samset & Volden, 2016). Mathur, Jugdev, and Fung (2014) found that leaders who supported project management processes experienced project and firm-level success. Specifically, project management integration was a strong significant predictor of both project and firm performance (Chang, 2017).

Effective Strategies to Improve Project Management at Health care Organizations

Executive directors of health care organizations use several strategies to improve project management. To receive an understanding of current strategies health care organizations executive directors use to improve project management success, I interviewed 10 participants with experience implementing successful project management strategies. Below is the discussion of some of the strategies participants found to be useful to enhance project management, including effective communication, project flexibility, team support, and best practices. In the findings below, P stands for a participant, and the number following the P represents the order of interviewed participants. For example, the first participant is P1. The data analysis from the interview indicated that refractive thinkers and leaders who can effectively implement a successful project management strategy could help their organizations achieve its mission by effective communication, improving project flexibility, and promoting team support and best practices.

Effective Communication Improved Project Management

Effective communication that improved project management was the first theme that emerged from exploring the participants' responses. Effective communication is an essential strategy to project management success (Dwivedi et al., 2015). Several participants (P1, P2, P4, and P9) described communication as one most critical element to project success. P1 said, "Number one is to have project management, the rest is communication." P9 agreed with P1 that a communication plan is critical for successful projects: "I think it's important to develop comprehensive change management and communication plan." P9 provided guidelines for project communication plans, which support this theme. Participants also discussed communication from multiple perspectives, including (a) the need for different communication methods, (b) the need for communication structure, and (c) the benefits of communication. Several participants (P1, P3, and P4) discussed the need for different communication methods and different audiences. P1 said that it's not one method or one communication because; senior executives needed a different level of an update than the project and operations management team. It's different communication at different times.

P9 provided documents that supported the idea, including formal presentations, emails, brochures, meetings, web communication, mailed letters, and on-site promotions. P3 also discussed various forms of communication he uses. Some examples were pull planning meetings, big room meetings, huddle boards, dashboards, and the company intranet. P4 indicated that repetition is necessary because, even though he may communicate multiple times, it could be the first time a stakeholder truly listens to his message. "That's something I had to learn throughout this process to be comfortable with just saying the same thing over and over because you have so many different stakeholders" (P4).

Participants also discussed the need to communicate using structured approaches. P7 indicated that there was a project stakeholder's weekly meeting while the project steer team met biweekly. P1 and P7 concurred on the importance of meeting regularly with different stakeholders. Additionally, P1, P7, and P2 indicated that the agendas for these meetings were standard from one meeting to the next meeting. P1's agenda included cost center reporting out on two topics, "One was to go over charge capture to make sure that all the charges are being captured as we expected. And the second was the rest of the revenue cycle."

Communication is important throughout the project lifecycle to address dynamic team issues. P4 said, "We had good communication throughout the project to make sure there was nothing that was creating any issues between the team." Communication can also help address current and future project roadblocks. P8 would rather have an early, candid, and potentially uncomfortable discussion about a project rather than allowing dissenting to fester and grow unaddressed. Conversely, communication can do more than mitigating issues. P4 also applied psychologists to help improve communication, which led to reduced staff anxiety, increased staff engagement, and additional opportunities for ongoing dialogue and updates about the project. Communication is an important theme and is present in all thematic categories.

Project's Flexibility Enhanced Project Performance

The project's flexibility improved enhanced project performance was part of the second theme that emerged from exploring the participants' responses. Eriksson, Larsson, and Pesämaa (2017) found that for infrastructure projects, flexibility enhanced project performance. P8 said that project leaders should make sure projects are persistent and flexible. Within this theme, the participants described flexibility regarding to stakeholder management, project leader and project management style, and communication. Flexibility in managing stakeholders is similar to the need for flexible communication strategies. However, stakeholder management is focused on connecting and building relationships with people.

P6 described, "To be an effective manager and an effective leader of people, you have to figure out the way to connect with people individually." Like communication strategies, to form relationships on an individual level, project leaders must be flexible in how they approach each stakeholder, "Relationship-based management is essential, and it's different, and you need to be flexible in how you apply it" (P6). Similarly, P8 admitted that project leaders could not satisfy 100% of everyone's wishes and desires. P10 described the flexibility needed to manage stakeholders as a *"yin and yang"* relationship, where project leaders need to engender a shared sense of project purpose while simultaneously outlining project limitations (P10).

Project leaders also need to be flexible in their project management approaches, an idea that was shared among multiple participants (P4, P6, and P9). P4 said that managers must adapt to the project management style or technique in different projects because there would be different stakeholders and different interactions. Similarly, P6 shared his experience of two different projects indicating that project management approaches vary with each project. P6 explained that the budgets, the risk, the quality, complexity, will dictate the need for the project planning materials. P9 stated that understanding the impact on the physician is a differentiator for projects in health care. These three leaders all believed that flexibility in dealing with stakeholders and maintaining positive relationships with them was an important project management strategy for achieving project success.

Project's Team Support Improved Project Delivery

Project's team support improved project delivery was the third theme that emerged. P3 expressed that support from the project leader precedes any project-related work. P9 described a strategy he uses to build his teams, which is that each team member has a voice in the subsequent team members that are selected to be part of the project, "So you might be the first person I brought on, now you're part of me picking the third team member. Then those three people are part of bringing on the fourth team member." By sharing the decision of who comprises the project team, P9 instilled a sense of ownership in the project's success.

Additionally, P8 thought of the important to question the viewpoints represented by the team members. P8 said, "There's equal toxicity on the total agreement and total disagreement; you have to find a blend there." P1 and P7 expressed a related idea of team composition, which is the importance of understanding the strengths and weaknesses of each team member. By knowing how each person can contribute to the team, P1 and P7 were alluding that project work can be assigned and completed effectively when individual strengths and weaknesses are considered. These findings relate to Böhm's (2013) assertion that project leaders should account for individuals' personalities and their work experiences as part of team management.

The participants recognized their role as project leaders to provide support and advocacy as an effective project management strategy. Showing support and advocacy is important, considering that insufficient project sponsorship by top-level leaders contributes to project failure (Dwivedi et al., 2015). P7 said he made sure to plan time to listen to his project team's concerns regularly to convey issues or resource needs on behalf of his team. P4 expressed the need to solicit project team feedback.

The presence of a project leader can be a form of demonstrating care and affirmation for the project team. P7 said that he met with his team at least once a week, but most of the time, more frequently than that. Similarly, P5 said "being on the ground with my team in very difficult times and not walking out the door at 5:00 showed my team how much I appreciate them." P9 was present with her team by making sure they had fun as a team, "I tend to feed people. I tend to use humor quite a bit, and relax with them and get them to understand this was really hard work." Project leader presence aligns with Badewi and Shehab (2016) description of leader attention being equivalent to leaders' level of project engagement.

Project Management Best Practices Enhanced Project Success

Project management best practices enhanced project success was the fourth theme that emerged. Badewi and Shehab (2016) concluded that applying project management practices are important to project success. To set clear expectations, project leaders need to use effective communication. P8 said that communication, behavioral standards, training, standard work, sharing stories, are related to best practices. Stanciu et al. (2016) indicated that communication is the lynchpin for project success because it provides a clear project direction.

Having clarity on what is part of the project and what is outside of the project documented helps set clear expectations for project stakeholders. Seven participants (P1-P3 and P6-P9) mentioned the importance of clarity as an effective project management strategy. For example, P3, P8, and P9 outlined the necessity to review and agree upon the conditions of satisfaction, or the project's goals, at the very beginning with all stakeholders involved. The participant's comments align with Collins, Parrish, and Gibson's (2017) findings that good scope definition can have a direct relationship to project success.

Burga and Rezania (2017) found that accountability went through various stages of translation via the project actors. In other words, project leaders interpreted how accountability for a particular project would be measured. P3 indicated the importance of accountability from both his project leader perspective and his teams and other stakeholders. P4 said that managers have a responsibility to carry on their shoulders, and it's their obligation as leaders of the project to acquiesce to the stakeholders and to determine how to move them, how to make them productive and how to have the project run efficiently.

Caldwell and Hayes (2016) found that self- awareness leaders increased leader effectiveness. Five participants (P1, P3, P4, P6, and P8) discussed the importance of self-awareness. The first type of self-awareness included leaders' understanding of their strengths and weaknesses. P4 shared his strengths and weaknesses by saying that he let experienced people lead, and he will follow from behind to promote strength, saying that he is comfortable with that. P4 understood the limitations of his expertise, and this self-awareness allowed him to set his pride aside and allow others to share their expertise. P4 said that his skills are seeing the big picture for ways to create efficiencies to operationalize the project.

Several participants (P2, P4, and P7) discussed the importance of taking action to gain project stakeholders' trust. P2 described the process as an "audition to get their trust." Additionally, P2 took steps to continue retaining trust, "Get those approvals and try to expedite resolution, avoid bureaucracy, avoid delays to highlight the importance of achieving project deliverables, which would result in stakeholders' confidence in the project leader."

Conclusion

Project managers can implement successful strategies to manage projects successfully in health care by using effective communication, project flexibility, team support, and best practices. The strategies shared by participants might help project managers achieve project success, increase productivity, and improve the organization's financial stability. Health care organizations managers need to consider and implement the above strategies to ensure that projects are successful. Implementing these strategies is less expensive than the costs associated with project failure. Recommendations include that health care organization' executive directors, scholars, and managers use the findings and recommendations of this study to gain new insight into project failure reduction strategies shared by experienced professionals. Health care organizations managers who can use a refractive thinking approach to implement effective project management strategies might bring long-term success to their organizations.

THOUGHTS FROM THE ACADEMIC ENTREPRENEUR

The Problem to be Solved:

- Reducing project failure in health care organizations
- Improving project's management by applying the required strategies

The Goals:

- Exploring the strategies that health care organizations projects managers use to prevent projects failure
- Improving organizational performance for sustainability

The Questions to Ask:

- What strategies do you use to prevent the project's failure and improve organizational performance for sustainability?
- What strategies were most effective in improving the project's success?
- What are a few positive outcomes from using the identified strategies for improving the project's management?
- What assessments do you use to assess the project's success and performance?

Today's Business Application:

- Effective project managers, who understand performance management can increase productivity and profitability, promote organizational commitment, which leads to organizational growth.
- The future of health care organizations depends on the project manager's ability to execute projects.
- Supportive project managers can increase organizational productivity and performance, which in turn promotes increased sustainability.

REFERENCES

Andreassen, H. K., Kjekshus, L. E., & Tjora, A. (2015). Survival of the project: A case study of ICT innovation in health care. Social Science & Medicine, 132, 62-69. doi:10.1016/j.socscimed.2015.03.016

Anthopoulos, L., Reddick, C. G., Giannakidou, I., & Mavridis, N. (2016). Why e-government projects fail? An analysis of the Health care.gov website. Government Information Quarterly, 33(1), 161-173. doi:10.1016/j.giq.2015.07.003

Badewi, A., & Shehab, E. (2016). The impact of organizational project benefits management governance on ERP project success: Neo-institutional theory perspective. International Journal of Project Management, 34, 412-428. doi:10.1016/j.ijproman.2015.12.002

Baird, S., & Boak, G. (2016). Leading change: Introducing an electronic medical record system to a paramedic service. Leadership in Health Services, 29(2), 136-150. doi:10.1108/LHS-04-2015-0012

Böhm, C. (2013). Cultural flexibility in ICT projects: A new perspective on managing diversity in project teams. Global Journal of Flexible Systems Management, 14, 115-122. doi:10.1007/s40171-013-0037-6

Boonstra, A. (2013). How do top managers support strategic information system projects and why do they sometimes withhold this support? International Journal of Project Management, 31, 498-512. doi:10.1016/j.ijproman.2012.09.013

Bresnan, M. (2016). Institutional development, divergence and change in the discipline of project management. International Journal of Project Management, 34, 328-338. doi:10.1016/j.ijproman.2015.03.001

Burga, R., & Rezania, D. (2017). Project accountability: An exploratory case study using actor–network theory. International Journal of Project Management, 35, 1024- 1036. doi:10.1016/j.ijproman.2017.05.001

Caldwell, C., & Hayes, L. A. (2016). Self-efficacy and self-awareness: Moral insights to increased leader effectiveness. Journal of Management Development, 35, 1163- 1173. doi:10.1108/JMD-01-2016-0011

Chang, J. T. (2017). Mutual monitoring of resources in an enterprise systems program. Project Management Journal, 48(1), 100-115. Retrieved from https://www.pmi.org/learning/publications/project-management-journal

Chatman, J. (2014). Culture change at Genentech: Accelerating strategic and financial accomplishments. California Management Review, 56(2), 113-129. doi:10.1525/cmr.2014.56.2.113

Collins, W., Parrish, K., & Gibson Jr., G. E. (2017). Development of a project scope definition and assessment tool for small industrial construction projects. Journal of Management in Engineering, 33(4), 04017015. doi:10.1061/(ASCE)ME.1943-5479.0000514

Crema, M., & Verbano, C. (2016). Identification and development of lean and safety projects. Safety Science, 89, 319-337. doi:10.1016/j.ssci.2016.07.007

Dao, B., Kermanshachi, S., Shane, J., Anderson, S., & Hare, E. (2016). Identifying and measuring project complexity. Procedia Engineering, 145, 476-482. doi:10.1016/j.proeng.2016.04.024

Duffield, S., & Whitty, S. J. (2015). Developing a systemic lessons learned knowledge model for organizational learning through projects. International Journal of Project Management, 33, 311-324. doi:10.1016/j.ijproman.2014.07.004

Dwivedi, Y. K., Wastell, D., Laumer, S., Henriksen, H. Z., Myers, M. D., Bunker, D., Srivastava, S. C. (2015). Research on information systems failures and successes: Status update and future directions. Information Systems Frontiers, 17(1), 143- 157. doi:10.1007/s10796-014-9500-y

Eriksson, P. E., Larsson, J., & Pesämaa, O. (2017). Managing complex projects in the infrastructure sector: A structural equation model for flexibility-focused project

Floricel, S., Michela, J. L., & Piperca, S. (2016). Complexity, uncertainty-reduction strategies, and project performance. International Journal of Project Management, 34, 1360-1383. doi:10.1016/j.ijproman.2015.11.007

Flynn, R., & Hartfield, D. (2016). An evaluation of a frontline led quality improvement initiative. Leadership in Health Services, 29, 402-414. doi:10.1108/LHS-11-2015-0039

Flyvbjerg, B. (2014). What you should know about megaprojects and why: An overview. Project Management Journal, 45(2), 6-19. doi:10.1002/pmj.21409

Foss, M. J., Frederiksen, L., & Rullani, F. (2016). Problem-formulation and problem-solving in self-organized communities: How modes of communication shape project behaviors in the free open-source software community. Strategic Management Journal, 37, 2589-2610. doi:10.1002/smj.2439

Garrety, K., McLoughlin, I., Dalley, A., Wilson, R., & Ping, Y. (2016). National electronic health record systems as 'wicked projects': The Australian experience. Information Polity: The International Journal of Government & Democracy in the Information Age, 21, 367-381. doi:10.3233/IP-160389

Grant, A. (2016). How to build a culture of originality: Anyone can innovate if given the opportunity and the support. Harvard Business Review, 94(3), 86-94. Retrieved from https://hbr.org

Harrington, H. J., & Frank, V. (2015). Cultural change management. International Journal of Innovation Science, 7(1), 55-74. doi:10.1260/1757-2223.7.1.55

Hassan, M. M., Bashir, S., & Abbas, S. M. (2017). The impact of project managers' personality on project success in NGOs: The mediating role of transformational leadership. Project Management Journal, 48(2), 74-87.

Hermano, V., & Martín-Cruz, N. (2016). The role of top management involvement in firms performing projects: A dynamic capabilities approach. Journal of Business Research, 69, 3447-3458. doi:10.1016/j.jbusres.2016.01.041

Hessler, P. (2016). Managing small and medium-sized capital projects. Chemical Engineering, 123(2), 54-57. Retrieved from http://www.chemengonline.com/

Hjelmbrekke, H., Hansen, G. K., & Lohne, J. (2015). A motherless child–Why do construction projects fail. Procedia Economics and Finance, 21, 72-79. doi:10.1016/S2212-5671(15)00152-5

Hussain, A., & Mkpojiogu, E. O. (2016, August). Requirements: Towards an understanding on why software projects fail. In F. A. A. Nifa, M. N. M. Nawi, &A. Hussain (Eds.), AIP Conference Proceedings (pp. 020046-1-020046-5). AIP Publishing. doi:10.1063/1.4960886

Hutchinson-Krupat, J., & Chao, R. O. (2014). Tolerance for failure and incentives for collaborative innovation. Production & Operations Management, 23, 1265-1285. doi:10.1111/poms.12092

Hyväri, I. (2016). Roles of top management and organizational project management in the effective company strategy implementation. Procedia - Social and Behavioral Sciences, 226, 108-115. doi:10.1016/j.sbspro.2016.06.168

Joslin, R., & Müller, R. (2015). Relationships between a project management methodology and project success in different project governance contexts. International Journal of Project Management, 33, 1377-1392. doi:10.1016/j.ijproman.2015.03.005

Karol, R. A. (2015). Leadership in the context of corporate entrepreneurship. Journal of Leadership Studies, 8(4), 30-34. doi:10.1002/jls.21350

Khattak, M. S., Mustafa, U., & Shah, S. S. (2016). Mapping project management competencies with different complexities for improving performance. Journal of Managerial Sciences, 10(2), 205-217. Retrieved from http://www.qurtuba.edu.pk/index.php/research/research-journals/journal-of- managerial-sciences

Kermanshachi, S., Dao, B., Shane, J., & Anderson, S. (2016). Project complexity indicators and management strategies: A Delphi Study. Procedia Engineering, 145, 587-594. doi:10.1016/j.proeng.2016.04.048

Killen, C. P., & Hunt, R. A. (2013). Robust project portfolio management: Capability evolution and maturity. International Journal of Managing Projects in Business, 6(1), 131-151. doi:10.1108/17538371311291062

Klein, L. (2016). Towards a practice of systemic change: Acknowledging social complexity in project management. Systems Research and Behavioral Science, 33, 651-661. doi:10.1002/sres.2428

Maqbool, R., Ye, S., Manzoor, N., & Rashid, Y. (2017). The impact of emotional intelligence, project managers' competencies, and transformational leadership on project success: An empirical perspective. Project Management Journal, 48(3), 58-75. Retrieved from https://www.pmi.org/learning/publications/project-management-journal

Mastrogiacomo, S., Missonier, S., & Bonazzi, R. (2014). Talk before it's too late: Reconsidering the role of conversation in information systems project management. Journal of Management Information Systems, 31(1), 44-78. doi:10.2753/MIS0742-1222310103

Mathur, G., Jugdev, K., & Fung, T. S. (2014). The relationship between project management process characteristics and performance outcomes. Management Research Review, 37, 990-1015. doi:10.1108/MRR-05-2013-0112

Mehta, S. J., & Ahmad, N. A. (2016). Aligning quality with the academic mission: A quality improvement and delivery science program in gastroenterology. Gastroenterology, 150, 543-546. doi:10.1053/j.gastro.2016.01.018

Meng, X., & Boyd, P. (2017). The role of the project manager in relationship management. International Journal of Project Management, 35(5), 717-728.

Moore, C. B., Payne, G. T., Autry, C. W., & Griffis, S. E. (2016). Project complexity and bonding social capital in network organizations. Group & Organization Management, 41, 1-35. doi:10.1177/1059601116650556

Oostveen, C. J., Ubbink, D. T., Mens, M. A., Pompe, E. A., & Vermeulen, H. (2016). Pre-implementation studies of a workforce planning tool for nurse staffing and human resource management in university hospitals. Journal of Nursing Management, 24(2), 184-191. doi:10.1111/jonm.12297

Project Management Institute (2018). A guide to the project management body of knowledge (PMBOK® Guide) (5th ed.). Atlanta, GA: Project Management Institute.

Ramazani, J., & Jergeas, G. (2015). Project managers and the journey from good to great: The benefits of investment in project management training and education. International Journal of Project Management, 33, 41-52. doi:10.1016/j.ijproman.2014.03.012

Reed, J. E., & Card, A. J. (2015). The problem with plan-do-study-act cycles. BMJ Quality & Safety, 25(3), 147-152. doi:10.1136/bmjqs-2015-005076

Samset, K., & Volden, G. H. (2016). Front-end definition of projects: Ten paradoxes and some reflections regarding project management and project governance. International Journal of Project Management, 34, 297-313. doi:10.1016/j.ijproman.2015.01.014

Sánchez, M. A., & Schneider, D. E. (2014). Project management, strategic management and sustainable development: A review of the literature. Revista Metropolitana De Sustentabilidade, 4(3), 28-49. Retrieved from http://www.revistaseletronicas.fmu.br/

Skoien, W., Page, K., Parsonage, W., Ashover, S., Milburn, T., & Cullen, L. (2016). Use of the theoretical domains framework to evaluate factors driving successful implementation of the accelerated chest pain risk evaluation (ACRE)

Stanciu, A. C., Condrea, E., & Zamfir, C. (2016). The importance of communication in quality management. Ovidius University Annals, Economic Sciences Series, 16, 393-396. doi:10.1016/j.sbspro.2014.04.127

Stoffers, J., & Mordant-Dols, A., (2015). Transformational leadership and professionals' willingness to change: A multiple case study in project management organizations. Human Resource Management Research, 5(2), 40-46. Retrieved from http://journal.sapub.org/hrmr

Valčić, S. B., Dimitrić, M., & Dalsaso, M. (2016). Effective Project Management Tools for Modern Organizational Structures. Annals of Maritime Studies 51(1), 131-145. Retrieved from http://hrcak.srce.hr/pomorski-zbornik

Van der Hoorn, B., & Whitty, S. J. (2017). The praxis of 'alignment seeking' in project work.

Volden, G. H., & Samset, K. (2017). Governance of major public investment projects: Principles and practices in six countries. Project Management Journal, 48(3), 90-108. Retrieved from https://www.pmi.org/learning/publications/project- management-journal

Zuo, J., Zillante, G., Zhao, Z. Y., & Xia, B. (2014). Does project culture matter? A comparative study of two major hospital projects. Facilities, 32, 801-824. doi:10.1108/F-02-2013-0014

About the Author...

Dr. Frank Musmar resides in Richardson, Texas. Dr. Frank is currently an adjunct professor at Louisiana International College and American Management and Technology University. Dr. Frank received his Doctorate of Business Administration (DBA) in Health care Management from Walden University in 2016, a Master of Science (MS) in Biotechnology Management from the University of Maryland in 2011 and Bachelor of Science (BS) in Agriculture from the University of Jordan in 1992.

Dr. Frank is the founder and the Lead Dissertations Consultant at Editors Dissertations and Thesis, founded on the ideals that helping students achieve their educational goals could bring positive social change.

Dr. Frank is also an active member of the Delta Mu Delta Honor Society and Golden Key International Honor Society.

He has published five journal publications: *The Effect of the Organizational Vision on Remote Employees Engagement, Factors Affecting Millennials Health care Employees Turnover, Job Embeddedness and Employee Retention in Health care, A Once-daily Oral Medication for Treatment of Cognitive Dysfunction in Down Syndrome,* and *Financial Distress at Nonprofit Organizations.* Additional work includes his dissertation: *Financial Distress in the Health Care Business.*

To reach Dr. Frank Musmar for information on professional editing or guest speaking, please visit his **websites:** http://www.editorsdissertationsandthesis.com or **e-mail: frankmusmar@gmail.com**

CHAPTER 3

Project Management's Considerations to Address Enterprise-wide Cyberthreats

Dr. Aaron Armour & Dr. Avideh Sadaghiani-Tabrizi

Analysis of organizational security postures and predictive analytics through use of big data could help to improve accuracy of the models, supporting to maintain resilience in threat environments with efforts to gain insights and counter cyber-attacks against unprecedented vulnerabilities of assets. The attention to details in information technology (IT) initiatives and implementation of security principles in every phase of enterprise-wide endeavors might help to reassure project managements' progress toward closure through prevention of private and protected data losses from cyber-crimes, beginning in the project's initiation phase. A cybersecure and aware ecosystem's reliance on mitigating risks from a variety of cyber-threats from a network of computers might benefit from preemptive measures to prevent risks of cyber-attacks in internetworking. A variety of attacks from a network of computers, compromised with malware that could form into botnets, present in many forms through ambiguity might cause an end-user's unintended attempt of installing the malware. The refractive approach in thinking to implement cybersecurity monitoring efforts might help attempts to protect privacy and vulnerabilities in threat environments. The use of data in automated detection work with machine learning (ML) algorithms and artificial intelligence (AI) learn from patterns of threats in behaviors, providing insights about presence of threats (Dynatrace, 2020). Accordingly, application performance management (APM), artificial intelligence operations (AIOps), cloud infrastructure monitoring, digital business and digital experience management (DEM) could advance knowledge in managing risks of cyberthreats on organizations with implementation of ML and analytics through deep-learning and neuro-nets.

Leveraging AIOps in detecting patterns necessitates collaboration to ease success and execution of projects. The assimilation of AI, cybersecurity monitoring, and expert systems could change the landscape of cyber-threats and vulnerabilities through algorithms and ML to propel automation, in enabling compliance. Complex projects, chains of criticality and efforts might require certified security project managers (CSPMs) implementation of decisions to incorporate changing skills within the landscape of a cybersecure ecosystem, which might benefit from a counterbalance of privacy with opportunities through implementation of artificial intelligence, machine-learning, and mathematical algorithms. Incorporating connected moving devices could present project management with numerous security risks of breaches and challenges in anomaly detection within neuro-networks of the emerging and interconnected world, evolution of FinTech, and zero-trust approach and cloud infrastructure (Das, 2018). Project managements' understanding of a variety of classifications, trends, regressions, deep-learning, and correlation of anomalies in joint finetuning and stacked neural networks (SNN) could help with modeling threats in detection of sentiments and unusual behaviors.

The implementation of convolutional neural network to classify and distinguish among images, cluster images and find similarities to recognize objects within scenes. Algorithms and classification of data could help to cluster nodes of raw data to train features of ML (Nicholson, 2019). Accordingly, the organizations' leaders' attempt to divert procedures for sophisticated monitoring systems and flash technology might help to alleviate the effect of data breaches through better governance and consideration of implementing resilient cyber-ecosystems and acquiring liability coverage. Many concerns over real privacy, compromise, compliance, use, misuse, and control of data might propel and alter collaboration beyond proof, in an environment that might "introduce new vulnerabilities, ranging from server and virtualization sprawl vulnerabilities to breaches, brute force attacks, and data theft" (Tabrizi, 2019, p. 59), through cybersecurity monitoring. Neural networks and AI could provide algorithms to correlate data in a timed-series deep learning for a classification to help ML to recognize patterns. The innovations in communication systems improve collaboration and organizational interactions by removing barriers in sharing information and increasing organization's sustainability, and business continuity to overcome the threats of catastrophic cybersecurity attacks, such as polymorphic malware that transform and conceal threats through AI.

The use of ensemble models could ease decisions from a combination of models in ML to improve the performance of projects. The continual examination of business continuity, productivity, and restoration plans might help organizations to achieve advancements in technologies in the competitive global economy, requiring management's effective governance strategies, evaluation of organizational security postures across the workforce influx, and mitigation to deal with risks (Ciampa, 2017). The different approaches to project management, warranting organizational business continuity might benefit from a clear project execution strategy to keep the business processes, communications networks, and operations resilient to threats of disruptions. Managers could use business intelligence (BI) as a planning strategy to combat cyberthreats and achieve success.

BI comprises the applications, infrastructure and tools, and best practices that enable access and analysis of information to improve and optimize decisions and performance. The BI tool consists of different planning strategies, which fit an organization's leaders' wants and needs, including all the different tools available for data analysis of business information and artificial intelligence technologies in companies. The accuracy of management's business decisions could benefit organizational data analysis efforts, in time to gain insights. The idea is to take away the guesswork.

Organizations' leaders could use BI to ascertain new revenue opportunities for competency in analyzing the company's data and gaining insights into vulnerabilities, and possibility of threats. Panorama (2018) stated that BI also helps managers to use key performance indicators (KPI). The use of KPIs could assist in the evaluation of an organization's activities, in which it engages (Panorama, 2018). This evaluation is done by capturing alerts and notifications each time there is a change in data regarding a specific KPI. Stratistics (2017) wrote the global BI market is expected to grow from $15.64 billion in 2016 to reach $29.48 billion by 2022 with a CAGR of 11.1% (Strattistics, 2017). Increasing of data analytics, raising the penetration of cloud technologies, and growing dependency on data in decision making are the factors fueling the market growth. Accordingly, increasing adoption of business intelligence in small and medium-sized enterprises is fostering the market growth which is why it is even more critical to address cyberthreats. Managers' use of strategies such as a good education to equip them with the ability to use good business practices when developing strategies for the organization, could benefit from incorporating business intelligence as a tool to address cyberthreats (Ilonen, 2018). Ilonen stated that the right amount of education could assist in finding the correct strategies for a business, and address threats because of the information technology-based nature of most business intelligence strategies (Ilonen, 2018). Choosing the right strategy and being innovative are essential to business survivability.

The predominance of projects' end-dates and strategy for the success of organizations might rely on the clear mission and vision of the company, in envisioning the systematic approaches to estimate schedules. Young eluded to the notion that managers must identify the direction and goals of the company in efforts of having success. The right strategy requires having a good team to execute the plan. Building the right team is key to any organization, which makes human capital even more critical. An organization is as successful as the people who work there, and human capital is an essential asset to the company. Accordingly, a successful organization depends on putting together a group of people who will bring ideas and a willingness to work in efforts of making the organization better can be the deciding factor on business success or failure (Young, 2015). The right team can be beneficial during meetings when creating ideas and goals for the strategic implementation of the dashboards.

The Need for Education

Business managers need a higher level of education that reach to a post-secondary degree in efforts of understanding strategic business concepts. The knowledge that will enrich business decisions could be imperative for overcoming challenges to implement better business practices. Education can generate learning outcomes that improve the business leader's understanding of business intelligence and company-wide security, as well as the understanding of themselves as leaders. Fayolle and Gailly (2015) stated even the top leaders within the organization should promote more education for the employees in an effort to get the most out of the company's human capital (Fayolle & Gailly, 2015). More top education leaders must take into consideration and understand what to consider for a business manager to decide to move on to a postsecondary educational establishment.

Choosing the Right Strategy

Every business leader must develop strategies that fit their company's mission and vision. The goals that are set in the beginning will be used to guide the company into the direction of the mission and vision statements. Choosing the right strategy is determined by the manager and the approach he or she is taking to accomplish specific goals. A considerable number of managers who could benefit from adopting more strategic planning strategies. Finding the right strategy for an organization takes knowledge and commitment to develop and sustain the plan. Implementation of the approach set during the beginning phase of the company could dictate the success of an organization. Managers who are developing enterprises should build on this concept for success and survivability.

Being Innovative

Business managers must be innovative to sustain a competitive edge. Technology changes rapidly every year, and managers must stay current with the change of this technology to remain up-to-date. An information technology profession or expertise is not necessary to execute some of the dashboard strategies, which are developed and used by small businesses although business intelligence dashboards are technology-based. An alarm processor that can help managers in decision-making with human decision making could help to bring in information. This information is what keeps the company current and moves the organization into the future.

The Right Team

Human capital is one of the most significant assets in an organization, in which an organization is as successful as the people comprise. Managers, owners, and employees all constitute the knowledge and labor behind accomplishing the organization's goals. Choosing the right team could be critical to making sure that goals are reached. Selecting the right team makes all the difference in achieving the mission and vision of the company. This is an excellent way to sustain competitive advantage, although there are many other ways of gaining this advantage. Business leaders in every industry should make a conscious effort to understand the importance of human capital because this is what makes up the organization.

Leadership

Effective formal mentoring programs could help to improve leadership competencies in most small businesses while developing socially responsible entrepreneurs who contribute to the economic well-being of businesses and communities, capitalizing on growth and financial education opportunities. Many small business managers have a significantly high level of leadership ability. Accordingly, leadership styles are vital to the success of an organization and businesses become more successful when strong leadership is present (McNamara, 2014). This ability contributes to success in developing great strategies for a business and sustaining the organization for many years.

The Emerging Threats and Challenges

Neural networks and the developments in artificial intelligence could contribute to suitability of quantum computing, training data and models with prospects of developments in bots to solve difficult problems or exploit communication networks, in breaking the public-key's cryptography infrastructure. The "quantum-resistant public-key cryptographic algorithms for standards" [algorithms need security against] "quantum and classical computers" (NIST, 2017, p. 1), interoperating with the existing communications protocols and networks. Cyber technology is the new battlefield, requiring private technology firms to maintain "security and peace" to work together with the government (Lis & Mendel, 2019, p. 45). Empirical design principles could help to formulate patterns to detect threats to deter vulnerabilities.

Resiliency

The exponential data-growth and big data threat surveillance agents could provide protection of organizational assets through efforts to anonymize and encrypt data. The genomic meta-data and federal supply chain are at risk, needing investments to "combat cybercrime and improve incident reporting" (Trump, 2018, p. v), by modernizing "electronic surveillance and computer crime laws," [reducing threats posed by] "transnational criminal organizations in cyberspace" (p. v). The variety of "anonymization and encryption technologies" (Lis, & Mendel, 2019), could (p. 9), help with restricting and obtaining "time-sensitive evidence," [for] "appropriate legal process" (p. 9). The resiliency of the cyber-ecosystem might present the demography of workplaces with investments in information security to go beyond protecting the businesses against cyber-attacks, with an approach to protect the privacy and organizational assets, strategically. The various views on technology use in the workforce might align with the differences in technology use and cohorts' stereotypes, placed on generational career aspirations of a multi-generational workforce (Ostrowski, 2018). Project managements' efforts to incorporate deep learning to judge between supervised learning, requiring labels to create patterns of recognition and clustering, or grouping in detecting similarities in unsupervised learning that do not require machine learning with labels might require knowledge of neural networks (Nicholson, 2019). Malware and known cyberattacks could configure to infect systems and inflict vulnerabilities to imperil victims.

Addressing Challenges

The application of blockchain technology could help CSPMs to build a platform to secure management of the non-kinetic aspects of cyberattacks in the cyberspace, and to improve upon cybersecurity of the critical infrastructure. The invisible state of digital assets' operating security platforms might need exercise of much scrutiny in protecting and managing safety, to reduce risks of loss and interference, in protecting organizational digital assets. The hash structure of the parent-to-child relationship in the blockchain security nodes could enable tracking and verifying hash-nodes of digital information patterns in the security platforms, to help in protecting information in storing securities assets and virtual currency transactions, efficiently. According to Lis and Mendel (2019), the growth of the blockchain attributes to blocks of data, which append and link, or chain to "previous block of data using a cryptographic hash function" (Lis & Mendel, 2019, p. 9).

In conclusion, the automation process of cognitive tasks, algorithms, big-data, and AI is beneficial to enterprises, in utilizing disruptive-technologies, cybersecurity, and AI in pre-training and classifying organizational networks' traffic to protect vulnerabilities against adversaries and many forms of frauds, social engineering threats, and incidents. The improvements in cooperation on data for security surveillance in detecting anomalies and monitoring risks of threats help with organizations' resiliency in classifying cybersecurity vulnerabilities, offering risk intelligence to detect threats in securing private and protected assets. Some of the most critical impressions for business intelligence strategies developing successful survivability is the vital need for education, building the right team, great leadership qualities, choosing the right strategy, and being innovative.

Managers and owners of small businesses in should strive for higher education. Being grounded in education enhances better business knowledge for practical concepts as well as strategic decision making. Understanding the importance of education in business is significant to the development process of an organization, and its longevity. Building the right team within an organization is important. Team building requires hiring the right employees and choosing the right individuals to complete specific tasks. Human capital being a significant part of an organization is the ideal reason why the team building is such an important aspect of organizational success. Every manager ought to develop great leadership qualities to gain a level of success in a company. Organizations are usually done by individuals having a great idea and build on that idea. However, it is important for an organization to put ideas into action, and managers communicate strategies and ideas to employee, effectively. Great leadership qualities assist in facilitating communication, and choosing the right strategies for a company's mission and vision is vital to the overall success of the organization, in which poor planning could lead to business failures. To be current and ahead of competitions could provide companies an innovative way to develop a successful company to compete with others within the industry.

THOUGHTS FROM THE ACADEMIC ENTREPRENEUR

The Problem to be Solved:

- Provide strategic solutions for securing information technology in not-for-profit and for-profit organization to offset dollars spent on projects, cost overruns, and cancelations.
- Ineffective team leadership that influences project performance.
- Assess the new threats of modern attacks.
- Provide rapid response to technological changes, and to re-align needs to counter volatilities in disruptive nature of technologies.

The Goals:

- Assess current organizational strategies to include project teams in an earlier stage of strategic planning
- Enhance team leadership skillset when managing multiple type compositions simultaneously

The Questions to Ask:

- How can nonprofit and for-profit businesses be augmented to improve project team's performance?
- How can evolvable strategy benefit organizational strategies for various not-for-profit and for-profit industries?

Today's Business Application:

- Assess the practically of Evolvability Strategy in existing organizational strategies.
- Treat team leadership as a practitioner's field and enhance skillset to accommodate managing multiple types of teams (traditional, virtual, and hybrid) concurrently.

REFERENCES

Ciampa, M. (2017). *Security+ guide to network security fundamentals*. Sixth Edition. Boston, MA: CompTIA.

Das, S. R. (2018). *The future of FinTech*. Santa Clara, CA: Santa Clara University. Retrieved from https://srdas.github.io/Papers/fintech.pdf

Dynatrace (2020). *What is Dynatrace?* © 2020 Dynatrace LLC. Retrieved from https://www.dynatrace.com/support/help/get-started/what-is-dynatrace/

Fayolle, A., and Gailly, B. (2015). The impact of entrepreneurship education on entrepreneurial attitudes and intention: Hysteresis and persistence. *Journal of Small Business Management, 53*(1), 75-93. doi:10.1111/jsbm.12065.

Ilonen, S. (2018). Identifying and understanding entrepreneurial decision-making logics in entrepreneurship education. *International journal of Entrepreneurial Behavior & Research*. 24. (1). 59-80.

Lis, P., & Mendel, J. (2019). Cyberattacks on critical infrastructure: An economic perspective, Economics and Business Review, 5(2), 24-47. doi: https://doi.org/10.18559/ebr.2019.2.2

McNamara, M. (2014). *Mentoring, coaching and action learning: interventions in a national clinical leadership development programme*. Retrieved from ProQuest Dissertation and Thesis Database. doi:10.1111/jocn.12461

The National Institute of Standards and Technology (2017). 2017 Annual report NIST/ITL cybersecurity program. U.S. Department of Commerce. Retrieved from https://doi.org/10.6028/NIST.SP.800-203

Nicholson (2019). *A beginner's guide to important topics in AI, machine learning, and deep learning*. A.I. Wiki. Retrieved from https://skymind.com/wiki/neural-network

Ostrowski, S. (2018, Sep). COMPTIA report examines the multi-generational workforce. CompTIA. Retrieved from https://www.comptia.org/about-us/news room/press-releases/2018/09/06/comptia-report-examines-the-multi-generational-workforce

Panorama. (2018). Basic benefits of business intelligence. Retrieved from: https://www.panorama.com/blog/10-simple-yet-powerful-benefits-business-intelligence/

Stratistics. (2017). Business intelligence (BI) – Global market outlook (2016-2022). Retrieved from: http://www.strategymrc.com/report/business-intelligence-bi-market

Tabrizi, A. S. (2019). The Refractive Thinker: Volume XVI – Generations: Strategies for managing generations in the workforce anthology. In C. Lentz (Ed.), *Chapter*

4: *Information technology security gap: Consideration of a diverse multigenerational cybersecure workforce* (pp. 59-79). Grayslake: IL: The Refractive Thinker Press.

Trump, D.J. (2018). National cyber strategy of the United States of America. Retrieved from https://www.whitehouse.gov/wp-content/uploads/2018/09/National-Cyber-Strategy.pdf

Young, D. B (2015). *Strategies for formally mentoring future business leaders.* Retrieved from ProQuest Dissertation and Thesis Database.

About the Authors...

Texas author Dr. Aaron Armour is an entrepreneur, certified business analyst, educator, and former athlete who holds several accredited degrees; Bachelor of Science (BS) in Business Development; a Masters of Business Administration (MBA) in Global Leadership; and a Doctor of Business Administration (DBA) all from Colorado Tech University. He is a United States Marine Corps Veteran who served honorably for 8 years. Dr. Aaron is also Lean Six Sigma Certified.

Dr. Aaron is currently the CEO of Armour Economic Solutions. Founded in 2015, AES is a consulting service that analyze, develop and implement solutions to business deficiencies to achieve clients' individual and business goals. The company also provide business analytical services by analyzing operational functions of businesses, identifying strengths and deficiencies, and providing recommendations. He is also a dissertation mentor and coach offering expertise as a professional writer.

Dr. Aaron has a wide-range of business development expertise with over 10 years of business analysis experience, including in-depth knowledge of strategic planning, business intelligence, and global leadership. He is an author known for his dissertation writings on *Exploring The Strategies Business Managers Need to Incorporate Business Intelligence Dashboards in a New Start African American Organization* that provided him the opportunity to gain expertise to facilitate significant improvements in the development of small to medium enterprises (SME's).

To reach Dr. Aaron Armour for information on refractive thinking, professional editing, or guest speaking, please **e-mail: draaronarmour@gmail.com**.

Dr. Avideh Sadaghiani-Tabrizi is from the Capital Region in upstate New York and holds several accredited degrees: a Doctorate of Management in Organizational Leadership with Specialization in Information Systems Technology (DM / IST) and a Master of Science in Computer Information Systems (MS / CIS) from the School of Advanced Studies of the University of Phoenix. Dr. Avideh Tabrizi is a security expert at the Office of Information Technology Services—Enterprise Monitoring and Support Group, participating in monitoring, research, design, development, and maintenance of statewide network system with over 20 years of service at the New York State government. She enjoys traveling and likes to engage in various physical fitness activities when possible.

Dr. Avideh Tabrizi's doctoral study entitled *Integrating Cybersecurity Education in K-6 Curriculum: Schoolteachers, IT Experts, and Parents' Perceptions* provided her the opportunity to gain a deeper understanding about academic needs of children and allowed her participation in multiple facets to suggest and facilitate improvements in the school district.

To reach Dr. Avideh Tabrizi for information on consulting or doctoral coaching, please **e-mail: drtabrizi2017@yahoo.com**.

CHAPTER 4

Preventing Wastes of Project Costs and Schedules Using Purposeful Knowledge Management

Dr. Cynthia J. Young

Organizations have various departments to sustain operations and ensure high profits and small losses. To support project knowledge sharing and transfer, leaders may incorporate a Project Management Office (PMO) into the organizational structure or have a construct implemented to manage portfolios, programs, and projects. Objectives of PMOs address is the management of cost and scheduling inherent in programs and projects. Managing a project is complicated when one considers operations, cost, scope, time, and resources, but organizations, especially project managers, are also managing stakeholder expectations throughout the project.

Purposeful knowledge management is not just expectation management of the customer or their requirements but the organization and, more specifically, the organization's senior leaders and the project teams. These expectations may intersect other company projects relying on sharing knowledge between projects in real-time to meet the expectations. Although no explicit requirement may exist to share or transfer lessons learned or provide copies of after-action reports (AAR) to fellow project managers, anticipating unspoken expectations are essential for sharing this information promptly to support other projects.

Thinking refractively, business leaders must be creative ensuring knowledge sharing and transference occurs through purposeful knowledge management practices. Sharing and transferring knowledge through purposeful knowledge practices means not waiting for the transition to another process group or the project close to share knowledge with just the C-suite while making every effort to ensure the culture of a project-driven organization is also a knowledge-sharing organization.

Preventing Wastes of Project Costs and Schedules Using Purposeful Knowledge Management

To ensure the success of an organization, each project team member must they are actively conducting purposeful knowledge management through sharing and transferring both tacit and explicit knowledge. Tacit knowledge is the knowledge a person knows what needs to be socialized to move to another person (Nonaka, 1994). Storytelling is a method of socialization of tacit knowledge, as well as coaching or knowledge sharing via Internet forums (Duffield & Whitty, 2016; Venkatraman & Venkatraman, 2018; Wijetunge, 2012). Explicit knowledge is codified knowledge (Nonaka, 1994) or in simpler terms, knowledge a person can acquire that has been searched, collected, and organized for access (Venkatraman & Venkatraman, 2018). Organizations use both tacit and explicit knowledge to support project creation, project execution, and the sharing and transferring of such expertise through lessons learned and AARs but should aim to use it purposefully to achieve project objectives for both the stakeholders and customers.

Using purposeful knowledge management ensures the organization can save time and money in their project management practices for the organization and its customers. In an organization, project teams may have the ethical and implied responsibility to share and transfer the knowledge for the projects in process and to support future projects. A barrier to knowledge transfer in project-based organizations is project teams appear to lack motivation to transfer knowledge with some researcher have determined a resistance to the knowledge itself (Bell, van Waveren, & Steyn, 2016). The Project Management Institute's (PMI®) Code of Ethics (2020) applies only to practitioners who are PMI members or non-members who hold a PMI® current certification and requires these practitioners to provide accurate information to include sharing bad news. In all projects, project teams must ensure the existence of social interactions and efforts to collaborate between project teams to ensure learning occurs (Hartmann & Doree, 2014).

Project Management Knowledge

Per the PMI® Project Management Book of Knowledge (PMBOK®), project teams use lessons learned registers to categorize and describe the project lessons learned and the impact, recommendations, and proposed actions for the issue recorded (Project Management Institute [PMI], 2017). In the PMBOK®, a lessons learned register is a record of the "challenges, problems, realized risks and opportunities, or other content as appropriate" (PMI, 2017, p. 104). During the closing phase, the project manager transitions the lessons learned from a record to a repository (PMI, 2017). PMI members (2017) identified project documents used by project managers in managing the project knowledge as assignments of project team members, the resource breakdown structure, source selection criteria, the stakeholder register, and all components of the project management plan.

Organizations must establish standardized lessons learned processes because a lack of standardization, especially for decentralized project teams who may not have daily contact at organizational headquarters, may lead to no sharing of the lessons learned across projects (van Grinsven & Visser, 2011). Chaves et al. (2015) created a model designed to support lessons learned from the PMBOK® process groups through web-based services. The researchers' intent was to promote a better understanding of project lessons learned for academics and practitioners of projects who use the PMBOK® (Chaves et al., 2015).

Integration of Knowledge Sharing and Transfer through the Project Process Groups

The inclusion of knowledge sharing and transfer through project process groups should be a circular item instead of a cleanup item at the end of the project or even at the beginning of the next project. Per the PMBOK® (PMI, 2017), outputs for managing knowledge management are any component updates of the project management plan or organizational process asset updates. Bell et al. (2016) cited similar stages in project-based organizations as initiate, develop, implement, operate, and close.

Even before the standard project process groups begin, a pre-planning stage of the project existed where the contract creation begins and provides overarching guidance on the requirements, desired end state, schedule framework, and budget. The arrangements developed in the pre-planning stages do not include methods to share or transfer information. A project manager may not be part of the project initiative process, depending on the organization's makeup. If an organization can support its project manager as part of this phase, this support may make the following project process groups more comfortable to manage for the customer.

Initiating Process Group

Initiating a project lays the groundwork for the project manager and the team. Without a formal knowledge requirement for costs and scheduling in the initiating phase due to these requirements specified in the planning process group, required processes to define those primary project elements (PMI, 2017). This groundwork is more than just project scope, cost, and scheduling. Project groundwork must also account for risks with the associated mitigations used in previous projects of similar scopes, costs, and schedules. Keeping the end state in mind is critical. When initiating a project, one of the first questions a project manager must ask is, has another project team completed a similar project in the past? The project manager must ask other questions such as:

- What were the outcomes of similar projects?
- Are lessons learned available in print?
- Were there any AARs completed?
- Is the project manager available to talk before starting this project?
- Are any of the team members available to help work on this project to ensure the same success assuming there was a success?

When organizational leaders prepare to start a project, review of prior projects of similar scope and costs should be identified and revisited for information that can be used to support the success of the upcoming project. Inclusion of a knowledge transfer mechanism should not be overlooked whether it is based on prior experience or is in print from a closing phase of a prior project (Bell et al., 2016). Knowledge transfer and sharing should be a part of an organizational standard for initiating any projects, whether internal or customer-based, to eliminate rework and avoid unnecessary wastes of costs and schedules.

Planning Process Group

Planning a project is, perhaps, the most challenging part of the entire project because the project team plans what the team will execute, and stakeholders will plan their work based on the project plan. Regarding costs and schedules, the PMBOK® prescribed preparing the schedule management, defining and sequencing the scheduling activities, developing the schedule, planning cost management, estimating costs, and determining the budget (PMI, 2017). The project manager includes communications management as part of the process group tasks (PMI, 2017). One unplanned change has the potential to throw the project plan off the original schedule and costs and thereby, extending the schedule or spending more than allotted. When planning a project, the project manager needs to be aware of what leaders of past projects encountered to know how fellow project managers address the issues.

- What have past teams experienced as far as funding or staffing issues?

- Are there any anticipated resource limitations?

Planning is more than just used for projects, but also for knowledge governance incorporation into the project plan (Pemsel, Soderlund, & Wiewiora, 2018). A plan must incorporate an understanding of the restrictions of the budgets and manpower to plan appropriately for the project and any risks associated with the execution of the plan. As project managers and the teams who help initiate the project support as part of the planning process group, knowledge gained from previous projects or projects still in execution can mitigate associated project risks before the plan transitions to the execution process group.

Executing Process Group

During project execution, project managers face multiple challenges. Rather than spend a significant amount of time addressing these issues as new challenges, project managers may want to speak to previous project managers to help define risk mitigations. Within the execution phase of a project, a significant challenge is maintaining the scope. Scope creep can occur at any time. Project teams usually see scope creep during the execution stage. Project teams and project managers want to do their best to support the customer, but they must consider cost and time. An increasing scope can throw the schedule and expenses off track. The risk of increased scope may result in having to tell the customer that the team cannot add additional work to the project. An increase in project scope can be detrimental to future projects the organization may support unless there is a knowledge-based solution available that the project manager can implement.

- Does the execution of the project have oversight beyond that of the project manager?
- Were there mitigated risks for costs or schedules? If so, how?
- Were these risks and mitigations shared throughout the organization?

The execution process group is where the project team experiences the realization of risks. Timely handling of risks and associated changes requires integration of the changes with required modifications and updates the project plans (Demirkesen & Ozorhon, 2017). Using a risk mitigation plan supports a team's ability to respond quickly to changes in that create uncertainties in projects because it requires teams to consider the risks in advance rather than in the middle of the project.

Monitoring and Controlling Process Group

As a project moves past the executing stage, project managers and their teams move into the monitoring and controlling phase of the project, which includes scope validation, controlling costs and schedules, and monitoring communications (PMI, 2017). Some methods of successful monitoring and controlling of processes include the requirements to match the needs of the organization, have established procedures, and associated guidelines (Bhatti & Ahsan, 2017). Inclusion of knowledge transfer practices into project planning and execution should extend into the monitoring and controlling process group (Young, 2016). This stage has the potential of complacency setting in. Complacency can give the project manager and their team a false sense of security that everything is going right if they do not carefully manage their costs and time.

- If the organization has a PMO, how timely is the information from the project going from the project manager to the PMO?

- Does the PMO have the knowledge to share and transfer lessons learned in real-time, or do they have to rely on the project manager to identify who needs the lessons learned?

- What should the team look for to share with other project teams?

- How should a project team share knowledge between shifts while working on a project?

Organizational oversight is part of the collaboration to support a project manager in monitoring the project progress. Lakemond, Bengtsson, Laursen, and Tell (2016) noted that knowledge matching provides coordination for ongoing communication and awareness in projects. Knowledge matching is essential to knowing when to share information as well as getting the information to right personnel.

Closing Process Group

When closing a project, project team members should provide documentation available for future project teams that may be responsible for items closely reflecting the project. When storing historic documentation in a place available to those teams, there must be lessons learned and AARs created and compiled. Per the PMBOK® (PMI, 2017), this documentation could be recorded per individual phase or contract line item vice just the entire project in a single document or event.

- Who is involved to close the project?
- Where are the historic documents stored? In a cabinet? On a shared drive?
- How is information from the closing of the project shared with other project teams?

The closing process group provides a path for an organization's project teams to locate knowledge to support future projects or projects in earlier process groups. Ebrahim, Mosly, and Abed-Elhafez (2016) determined that devising a process to link project documents and reports makes the handover and closeout easier. Use of the closing process group also supports a cyclical nature of knowledge management where project teams can share and transfer knowledge.

Process Theory

Niederman, Muller, and March (2018) evaluated a concept regarding how process theory can support knowledge accumulation and gathering and concluded that the method has *significant promise* to support the lessons learned collected throughout a project. Niederman et al. also identified anecdotal knowledge in project management to support an advanced testable theory base. Knowledge brokering could potentially tie to this conceptual framework. Knowledge brokering includes knowledge management and knowledge translation and exchange as two of its seven activities (Beratan, 2019). Project managers and their teams can begin building the knowledge to support their projects through other projects. Knowledge brokering can help organizational change by integrating the formal aspects of project knowledge with storytelling and act as a management tool (Wijetunge, 2012). Storytelling can be more attractive to the listener and gives them a chance to informally discuss the project and interact with the person who experienced the project, asking clarifying questions throughout the story.

Project Costs and Schedules

Time and money are two of the items evaluated throughout the life cycle of a project using the process of earned value management (EVM). Projects succeed and fail, not just based on an organization's ability to meet the requirements of schedule and costs, but by learning from previous projects throughout all project phases. Using EVM provides a quantitative analysis of where the project rests within the scheme of the project. Project managers must use EVM to help mold their decisions and decide where to put the efforts to either maneuver costs and schedules back on track or maintain the current relationship with the targets.

Whether the job is transactional or transformational, project managers must provide direction that will help the team achieve the EVM rating for cost and schedule. If project managers cannot reduce costs or save time later in the project timeline, the project could fail or at least be a complicated project to complete adequately for the customer.

When managers consider saving time and money in organizational project management, knowledge management is not always considered a tool to accomplish those savings. Managers must share project information continually and to make sure stakeholders understand the status of time and money with the requirements. Knowledge which is shared and transferred purposefully through a standard process using lessons learned AARs should also include other methods such as storytelling and shadowing due to various methods of learning (Wijetunge, 2012). If organizations cannot accurately transfer this information, holding onto the associated data does not help the organization, but acknowledging and using various methods to share and transfer information can support learning throughout the organizational enterprise.

Expert judgment is based on tacit knowledge, knowledge management, information management, interpersonal, and team skills are methods of sharing and transferring project knowledge (PMI, 2017). Sharing and transferring knowledge requires managerial direction during projects to prevent knowledge from getting forgotten as teams work through the project planning phases. Using expert judgment can mean that somebody can read something and speak about it because they have lived it as well, or they can have a degree in the topic or have managed a project with the same task.

The term knowledge management is quite nebulous in this aspect. Knowledge management may be viewed as information management if people are not adequately trained on how to manage the knowledge within their organization. The last part, interpersonal and team skills, is the most exciting and adaptable part of knowledge management that project managers must address to have solid team communication. A barrier to knowledge sharing may be because no one person is the same on one team to the next and the team skills can shift from project to project even if the team is the same from one project to another project. Leaders must address ensuring knowledge management supports innovation and corporate culture since barriers and identification of knowledge gaps may exist and prevent knowledge sharing and knowledge transfer (Young, 2016). Within an organization, leaders as well as their teams must accept that knowledge management practices are only as successful as the ability to support through interpersonal relationships and team building.

Sharing and Transferring Project Knowledge

Project support work encompasses the use of spreadsheets and other various documents. Project managers work with people whether it be individuals or teams. Interpersonal skills are essential for project success since trust across cross-functional project teams and prior relationships must exist for effective communication between teams (Buvik & Rolfsen, 2015) to sharing direction across accurately and for receiving information back as a project manager. Similarly, the inability to share information can also be the same between team members who have worked as teammates on previous projects. Interpersonal skills are not a given. Emotional connections within the team encourage team members to complete a job as best as possible. Paying somebody to do a job is not the same as encouraging a person to perform well at a job, but there are methods of sharing knowledge within a project team, between project teams, and throughout an organization.

Organizations can share and transfer project knowledge through lessons learned, communities of practice (CoPs), and AARs.

Lessons Learned

Ferrada, Nunez, Neyem, Serpell, and Sepulveda (2016) identified that project members from a construction project did not integrate lessons learned into subsequent projects and developed a lessons learned system to incorporate knowledge management through a mobile cloud-shared workspace. When using social media, lessons learned to continue to be a challenge to manage in the project management community (Winter & Chaves, 2017). Project managers may use software for organizational knowledge management, while others rely on sharing lessons learned and training after the event to convey knowledge gained from a project (Young, 2016).

Duffield and Whitty (2016) suggested sharing lessons learned through social media, special interest groups, meetings, and storytelling forums. Goffin and Koners (2011) conducted 30 interviews and elicited 273 lessons learned based on tacit knowledge during new product development. Goffin and Koners tied tacit knowledge from four lessons learned regarding project budgets, problem-solving, time schedules, and product specification change, but were unable to capture all implicit knowledge learning through the interviews of personnel of the five companies involved in the study.

Communities of Practice

A CoP is a group of like-minded people who foster organizational knowledge sharing (Alijuwaiber, 2016). Venkatraman and Venkatraman (2018) classified four CoP implementations: Internal CoP that is internal to the organization, networked organizational

CoPs based on a network of collaborations, CoP networks based on formally knowledge sharing, and self-organized CoP which is an informal network maintained as ad-hoc relationship. CoPs may have a lead to support the direction of the CoP and a method of tracking information shared to include minutes taken in CoP meetings or calls.

After-Action Reports

AARs are tools used by teams to share the outcome of a project. Crowe, Allen, Scott, Harms, and Yoerger (2017) investigated what made good and bad AARs through open-ended interview questions to AAR attendees through two studies. The research indicated that open-ended questions resulted in strong agreement with facilitation requirements for useful and unusable AARs where AARs were a venue for team building with potential for enhancing an environment for safety (Crowe et al., 2017). Project teams need to communicate AARs in a public environment and not just in a management meeting setting. We are more than just the current team who can read the information or participate in the AAR debrief. An AAR is only as good as the participants asking the questions. If a team cannot communicate information that is usable by personnel outside of their team as well as those on their team for future events, then why do it? Within all branches of the military, personnel are expected to share knowledge and lessons learned while being innovative with processes and procedures for organization and project success (Young, 2016).

Recommendations

The following recommendations may aid an organization and project teams begin working projects knowing the lessons learned and AARs of prior projects as well as those projects in progress:

Although a PMO would share knowledge between project

managers and their teams, it may be more fruitful for an organization to operate using CoPs. These CoPs would have personnel assigned from each project team so they would be closer to the issues than the PMO. When there is more ownership in the CoP membership than the PMO, CoP members may gain more knowledge and take the knowledge gained back to their respective project teams as well as including the PMO in the discussions.

Use lessons learned at the beginning of the project before the start of the initiating phase of a project when the organization is making its considerations for the prevention of recurring problems. To begin this process, consider using a lessons learned database (Ferrada et al., 2016) so organizations can support teams to review the database before the start of the project initiation. Careful management of the database ensures a database does not have duplicative entries or retain outdated information. A lessons learned database should not be a dumping ground for all projects and require regular curation by a knowledge manager or someone familiar with using lessons learned. Consider using a one-sentence issue, one or two paragraph discussion to describe while the issue is problematic, and a one-paragraph recommendations format for lessons learned.

Do not just require AAR submissions. Ensure AARs are part of the standard project closing process. Present the AAR to the C-suite and the project teams together so there can be a question and answer session to ensure clarification of any issues for all involved with the projects. If possible, have other organizational project managers present to provide insight that may help the teams with projects in progress. Publish the AAR, where the organization has access to it to review the AAR as needed.

Project managers should not forget to share information. Sharing information throughout the organization is especially important for experienced project managers because project managers and their teams may have addressed complicated challenges and failed. When sharing experiences, what a project team learns is just as valuable as sharing itself. The sharing events are the teachable moments to allow people to learn and remember what happened, what causes the problem, and how they conquered the issue.

Conclusion

Projects come with challenges that can increase costs or extend project schedules. Organizations must have processes implemented to share lessons learned and AARs. When organizational leadership and project managers do not manage the knowledge of problems and the associated corrections, the problems may occur later in concurrent or future projects. Incorporating any of the recommendations of using CoPs, lessons learned throughout the project, sharing AARs outside of the standard grouping of people, or just using your intuition to ensure the teachable moments are not missed are important to minimizing costs and staying on or ahead of schedule and prevention of the associated waste of costs and schedules.

As a previous program manager and division manager, it is clear that project successes and failures must be shared for other projects to be successful. Success is not always immediate. As knowledge sharing and transfer becomes part of the organizational culture and leaders and managers make the knowledge management expectations known, project teams can see the benefits of the process. As it becomes part of an organization's culture and with that, project management processes, thinking refractively through knowledge management supports the entire team from organization through the external stakeholders to include the customers. Knowledge management takes effort and refractive thinking to use the different methods of sharing and transferring knowledge for the benefit of the entire team.

THOUGHTS FROM THE ACADEMIC ENTREPRENEUR

The Problem to be Solved:

- Ensuring knowledge loss does not occur because of waiting until the end of a project to document it to share and transfer it.

The Goals:

- Make lessons learned available to other project managers and their teams throughout the project and after the project closes.
- Publicly hold open AAR events to allow personnel other than only the project team and management to attend.
- Document and make the AAR available for review for those who cannot participate in the event.
- Encourage knowledge sharing and transfer as part of the organizational culture.

The Questions to Ask:

- How do organizations prioritize knowledge sharing and knowledge transfer?
- What methods are available to share and transfer tacit and explicit knowledge to function across projects in different verticals?

Today's Business Application:

- Ensure knowledge sharing and knowledge flow permits for real-time problem-solving.
- Ensure knowledge is shared outside of verticals, staying away from internal vertical-only knowledge sharing.

REFERENCES

Alijuwaiber, A. (2016). Communities of practice as an initiative for knowledge sharing in business organisations: A literature review. *Journal of Knowledge Management, 20*, 731-748. doi:10.1108/JKM-12-2015-0494

Bell, L., van Waveren, C. C., & Steyn, H. (2016). Knowledge: Sharing within the project-based organization: A knowledge-pull framework. *South African Journal of Industrial Engineering, 27*(4), 18-33. doi:10.7166/27-4-1580

Beratan, K. K. (2019). Improving problem definition and project planning in complex natural resource management problem situations using knowledge brokers and visual design principles. *Ecology and Society, 24*(2). doi:10.5751/ES-10815-240231

Bhatti, M. W., & Ahsan, A. (2017). Global monitoring and control: A process improvement framework for globally distributed software development teams. *Journal of Global Information Technology Management, 20*(10), 43-63. doi:10.1080/1097198X.2017.1280303

Buvik, M. P., & Rolfsen, M. (2015). Prior ties and trust development in project teams: A case study from the construction industry. *International Journal of Project Management, 33*, 1484-1494. doi:10.1016/j.ijproman.2015.06.002

Chaves, M. S., de Araujo, C. C. S., Teixera, L. R., Rosa, D. V., Junior, I. G., & Nogueria, C. D. (2015). A new approach to managing lessons learned in PMBOK process groups: The Ballistic 2.0 model. *International Journal of Information Systems and Project Management, 4*(1), 27-45. doi:10.12821/ijispm040102

Crowe, J., Allen, J. A., Scott, C. W., Harms, M., & Yoerger, M. (2017). After-action reviews: The good behaviors, the bad behavior, and why we should care. *Safety Science, 96*, 84-92. doi:10.1016/j.scci.2017.03.006

Dermirkesen, S., & Ozorhon, B. (2017). Impact of integration management on construction project management performance. *International Journal of Project Management, 35*, 1639-1654. doi:10.1016/j.ijproman.2017.09.008

Duffield, S. M., & Whitty, S. J. (2016). Application of the systemic lessons learned knowledge model for organizational learning through projects. *International Journal of Project Management, 34*, 1280-1293. doi:10.1016/j.ijproman.2016.07.001

Ebrahim, M. A-B., Mosly, I., & Abed-Elhafez, I. Y. (2016). Building construction information using GIS. *Arabian Journal for Science and Engineering, 41*, 3827-3840. doi:10.1007/s13369-015-2006-1

Ferrada, X., Nunez, D., Neyem, A., Serpell, A. & Sepulveda, M. (2016). A lessons learned system for construction project management: A preliminary application. *Procedia–Social and Behavioral Sciences, 226*, 302-309. doi:10.1016/j.sbspro.2016.06.19

Goffin, K., & Koners, U. (2011). Tacit knowledge, lessons learnt, and new product development. *Journal of Product Innovation Management, 28*, 300-318. doi:10.1111/j.1540-5885.2010.00798.x

Hartmann, A., & Doree, A. (2015). Learning between projects: More than sending messages in a bottle. *International Journal of Project Management, 33*, 341-351. doi:10.1016/j.ijproman.2014.07.006

Lakemond, N., Bengtsson, L., Laursen, K., & Tell, F. (2016). Match and manage: The use of knowledge matching and project management to integrate in collaborative inbound open innovation. *Industrial and Corporate Changes, 25*(2), 333-352. doi:10.1093/icc/dtw004

Niederman, F., Muller, B., & March, S. T. (2018). Using process theory for accumulating project management knowledge: A seven-category model. *Project Management Journal, 49*(1), 6-24. Retrieved from http://www.pmi.org/PMJ

Nonaka, I. (1994). A dynamic theory of organizational knowledge creation. *Organization Science, 5*, 14-37. Retrieved from http://orgsci.journal.informs.org

Pemsel, S., Soderlund, J., & Wiewiora, A. (2018). Contextualising capability development: Configurations of knowledge governance mechanisms in project-based organizations. *Technology Analysis & Strategic Management, 30*, 1226-1245, doi:10.1080/09537325.2018.1459538

Project Management Institute (PMI). (2020). *Code of ethics and professional conduct.* Retrieved from https://www.pmi.org/-/media/pmi/documents/public/pdf/ethics/pmi-code-of-ethics.pdf?v=5b0f0983-6467-4d7d-9aae-577fbac4d-4b3&sc_lang_temp=en

Project Management Institute (PMI). (2017). *A guide to the project management body of knowledge (PMBOK® guide)* (6th ed.). Newtown Square, PA: Project Management Institute.

Wijetunge, P. (2012). Organizational storytelling as a method of tacit-knowledge transfer: Case study from a Sri Lankan university. *The International Information and Library Review, 44*(4), 212-223. doi:10.1016/j.iilr.2012.09.001

Winter, R., & Chaves, M. S. (2017). Innovation in the management of lessons learned in an IT project with the adoption of social media. *International Journal of Innovation (UI Journal), 5*(2), 156-170. doi:10.5585/iji

van Grinsven, M. V., & Visser, M. (2011). Empowerment, knowledge conversion and dimensions of organizational learning. *The Learning Organization, 18*(5), 378-391. doi:10.1108/09696471111151729

Venkatraman, S. & Venkatraman, R. (2018). Communities of practice approach for knowledge management systems. *Systems, 6*, 36, doi:10.3390/systems6040036

Young, C. J. (2016). *Knowledge management and innovation on firm performance of United States ship repair* (Doctoral dissertation). Available from ProQuest Dissertations and Theses database. (UMI No. 10042541)

About the Author...

Dr. Cynthia J. Young resides in Chesapeake, Virginia. Dr. Cindy holds several accredited degrees; a Bachelor of Arts (BA) in English Language and Literature from the University of Maryland, College Park; two Masters of Business Administration (MBA), one in e-commerce and one in advanced management studies, from Trident University International; and a Doctorate of Business Administration (DBA) from Walden University.

Dr. Cindy is the President / CEO of CJ Young Consulting specializing in helping organizations to integrate knowledge management into their daily operations as well as a Theater Mission Planning Center Curriculum Developer and Instructor with Leidos, a defense contracting company. She is a retired Surface Warfare Officer with 23 years in the U.S. Navy. She is a past-Chair of American Society for Quality, Tidewater, Section 1128, and a member of the Project Management Institute, Golden Key International Honor Society, and Delta Mu Delta International Business Honor Society.

Dr. Cindy holds professional certifications as a Project Management Professional, a Lean Six Sigma Master Black Belt, and as an ASQ-Certified Manager of Quality / Organizational Excellence. Her doctoral study, *Knowledge Management and Innovation on Firm Performance of United States Ship Repair*, provided her the opportunity to gain additional professional and academic expertise to facilitate improvements in organizational knowledge management. She is also the author of *Chapter 3: Using Leadership to Improve Firm Performance Through Knowledge Management* from *The Refractive Thinker®: Vol XI: Women in Leadership* and *Chapter 4: Ensuring Prosperous Knowledge Flow from the Silent Generation Through Generation Z in a Global Workforce* from *The Refractive Thinker®: Vol XVII: Managing a Cultural Workforce: The Impact of Global Employees*.

To reach Dr. Cynthia J. Young for additional information or guest speaking, please visit her on **LinkedIn: https://www.linkedin.com/in/drcindyyoung/** or **e-mail: cjyoung@cjyoungconsulting.com**

CHAPTER 5

Project Solutions: Managing the Remote Pieces of Offshoring and Onshoring

Dr. Ivan Salaberrios

Although the precise definition of offshoring, also known as business process outsourcing (BPO), sub-serving, or outsourcing, is not agreed upon, researchers and experts consistently use these terms to collectively and interchangeably refer to the process of contracting out an in-house business function to a third-party or external provider. (Manning, Massini, & Lewin, 2008). This way of conceptualizing offshoring and outsourcing as one and the same thing has caused considerable confusion. Although the principles between these two terms (i.e., outsourcing and offshoring) are similar, they refer to slightly different things and have implications and repercussions.

A key aspect of project management is sourcing. Project managers have to manage people who are located in other countries. Whether the resource is one person or an entire call center, project management relies on offshoring and outsourcing. Project managers need to know how manage offshore resources. Project managers need to know when outsourcing should be used as a solution to a business problem and vice versa. Knowing how to manage remote resources located offshore is a very nice attribute for a project manager. A project manager needs to adapt and develop management skills in order to manage offshore resources.

Project managers who are responsible for managing outsourced suppliers or individual resources can benefit from this chapter.

Outsourcing, as used in the popular press and the academic literature, refers to a strategy used by companies that involves contracting services of a third-party service provider or external agency to manage a specific project or set of business processes. In this sense, outsourcing occurs when two companies enter into a contractual agreement that involves the exchange of payments and services, with one firm allowing an external firm to handle its functions. Outsourcing does not involve the physical transfer of assets rather the delegation or assignment of services to another third-party service provider located in another country or region.

Palugod (2011) emphasized that the outsourcing arrangement allows another company to perform some functions of another company previously undertaken in-house or internally. For example, a company can enter an outsourcing arrangement with another company allowing it to manage its production processes, or finance and payroll services. According to Palugod, an outsourcing arrangement, as used today, refers to the outsourcing of business process and information technology (IT) services or the transfer of operational services, rather than manufacturing processes with an aim of reducing services supplied internally and shortening the supply chain. Palugod added that most companies engage in an outsourcing arrangement using vertical integration to perform their IT and business processes. Palugod believed that the aim of outsourcing is to save fixed, production, and development costs often achieved by the company focusing on strengthening its research and development.

Other related terms are *the fragmentation of global value chain, international insourcing, international outsourcing, trade in tasks, international outsourcing,* and *global production sharing* which all describe the location of various stages of production processes (Stehrer et al., 2012).

Outsourcing: The Business and Academic Perspective

Offshoring, as used in business and the academic literature, refers to the business' ability to outsource to other companies located in another country (Manning et al., 2008). The study indicates the emphasis of offshoring is on the relocation of operating activities to another country. Supporting this view, Sethupathy (2013) advanced that offshoring involves a company undertaking a service process or function in a foreign country. In this business arrangement, another company undertakes the function of a subsidiary of the company located in another country, also referred to as shared service division or a captive company. The function or process can be termed both *outsourced* and *offshored* when performed by a third-party company. In view of these perspectives, offshoring and outsourcing refer to different yet related processes.

Other related terms have emerged that capture the different aspects of the complex relationship between networks and economic organizations including offshore outsourcing; strategic outsourcing; multi-sourcing; far-shoring, and nearshoring (Manning et al., 2008; Norwood et al., 2006). These terms are important for project managers to know as they manage these offshore resources.

Nearshoring is a subdivision of offshoring used to refer to the practice of transferring or outsourcing information technology processes to less expensive companies located in a country that shares the geographical border with the target company. In multi-sourcing, the target company contracts or procures IT operations and technology infrastructure to multiple vendors in combination with the elements of IT provided internally.

Far shoring is a special form of offshoring which involves transferring or outsourcing information technology processes to less expensive companies located far from the target company's country. This form of offshoring is the direct opposite of nearshoring.

Onshoring—the opposite of offshoring—is the practice of relocating business processes or functions to a lower-cost location within the country's national borders. The concept behind onshoring is that relocating business processes or functions near customers may foster the establishment of closer working agreements and facilitate the faster provision of services tailored to suite market needs. Politicians argue that through onshoring, a company can improve its cost structure, foster flexibility, and improve communication and coordination of production.

Offshore outsourcing as used in this chapter refers to the strategic practice involving a company or firm contracting a third-party supplier to undertake the work in another or foreign country. A project manager needs to know how to adapt and develop their management skills to effectively manage these strategies.

Business Perspective: Outsourcing Risks

Many firms operating globally remain concerned about the risk of offshore outsourcing (Ghoshal, 1987). Risks of outsourcing approached economics, health care, or business perspectives. From the business perspective, different researchers identified and categorized outsourcing risks differently (Barthelemy, 2001; Earl, 1996; Herath & Kishore, 2009; Kotabe & Murray, 2004; Willcocks, Feeny, & Lacity, 2004; Quinn & Hilmer, 1994; Rubin, 2009). For Herath and Kishore (2009), offshore outsourcing risks are reduced product quality, loss of control over suppliers, and undesirable consequences. From the supply chain business perspective, Li and Barnes (2008) identified the risk of offshore at phase 1 and phase 2 of the outsourcing process.

Risks at Phase 1 (Ex-tante) Contract Stage

Phase 1 is the ex-ante contract phase. Li and Barnes (2008) noted that risks at ex-ante contract phase occur during contract development, decision-making, and supplier selection stages of the outsourcing process. According to Li and Barnes (2008), during this phase, notable risks are supply market environment risks, namely economic risks, cultural risks, and political risks. The political risks identify as environmental regulations and laws, unpredictable changes in labor, and political instability (Ellram, Tate, & Billington, 2008; Graf & Mudambi, 2005). Language and cultural barriers are potential risks to offshore outsourcing (Graf & Mudambi, 2005; Kakumanu & Portanova, 2006; Schniederjans & Zuckweiler, 2004). According to Schniederjans and Zuckweiler (2004), language barriers may lead to conflicts, misunderstanding, and delays by causing communication difficulties between suppliers and the firm.

By contrast, cultural differences such as decision-making styles, social norms, and religion can undermine collaborative efforts during the outsourcing process and hinder the supplier and client firms from establishing trust (Graf & Mudambi, 2005). Economical risks associate with variability in the currency exchange rate and an inflation rate that impact negatively on the outsourcing firms' financial performance (Dhar & Balakrishnan, 2006). According to Ellram et al. (2008), these macro environmental risks are exceptionally important when making outsourcing consideration and selecting vendors in certain regions.

Risks During the Ex-post Contract Phase

Risks during the ex-post contract phase occur during supplier management stage of the offshore outsourcing process (Lee & Kim, 1999). According to Haried and Ramamurthy (2009), supplier management is an important aspect during the ex-post contract phase of offshore outsourcing, yet various risk lies at this stage. Risks at this stage identify as experience risks; opportunistic behaviors and insufficient capability on the part of the supplier; and unintentional knowledge leakage and conflicts (Costa, 2001). Bahili and Rivard (2003) find the firm's lack of experience in offshore outsourcing can lead to loss of control over external suppliers, and unexpected management and transaction costs. Studies indicated identifying risks of escalating costs linked to unexpected management costs and transactions (Cavusgil, Yaprak, & Yeoh, 1993; Mahnke, Lucas, & Vang, 2005). For Ellram et al. (2008), firms that engage in offshore outsourcing may experience risks related to outsourcing expertise and experience and internal uncertainty in relation to outsourcing requirements. These risks could increase the difficulty for a firm to foresee problems such as hidden costs, management conflicts, and incomplete contract specifications during the outsourcing process (Dhar & Balakrishnan, 2006; Earl, 1996).

Identifying unresolved conflicts as a possible risk during offshore outsourcing, Quinn and Hilmar (1994) indicated that unresolved conflicts during the ex-post contract phase may cause firms to lose connection with their suppliers. Other researchers held that supplier's opportunistic behaviors and lack of capability can lead to quality issues, delayed delivery, and longer lead time periods during offshore outsourcing (Enderwick, 2008; Herath & Kishore, 2009). As described by Aron and Singh (2005), the supplier's opportunistic behavior refers to action taken by the supplier with the view to maximize profits. According to Barthelemy (2003), supplier's opportunistic behavior causes the wrong selection on the part of the purchasing firm. Barthelemy (2003) further noted the supplier's opportunistic behavior could negatively impact outsourcing management at this stage of outsourcing. Williamson (2008) believed that asset specificity is a potential risk during the outsourcing management stage of offshore outsourcing.

In line with Williamson (2008), McIvor (2009) advanced that managing outsourcing relationships requires firms to make significant relationship-specific investments, such as investments in human and physical assets. Herath and Kishore (2009) noted that asset specificity can cause firms to be in a *lock-in* situation especially where only a few qualified suppliers are available. Herath and Kishore (2009) increased transaction costs during outsourcing management may also play a role in increasing the risk of escalating cost. Other researchers identified firms' lack of expertise and inexperience as the possible risk during the ex-post contract phase, and that these issues may cause conflicts between suppliers and client firms (Mohr & Spekman, 1994; Haried & Ramanurthy, 2009). Haried and Ramanurthy (2009) noted conflicts between the supplier and the client firms during the ex-post contract phase triggers several factors, namely lack of commitment and trust, unbalanced information, and miscommunication. As argued by Morgan and Hunt (1994), poor conflict resolution at this stage could lead to relationship termination and other destructive outcomes. For other researchers (Aron & Singh, 2005; Kakumanu & Portanova, 2006) an unintended knowledge leak is one of the key risks during offshoring outsourcing. Aron and Singh (2005) clarified that an unintended knowledge risk may occur when suppliers try to steal or misuse proprietary knowledge for other reasons and purposes. Das and Teng (1996) categorized risks in offshoring outsourcing into two: performance risk and relational risks.

As described by Das and Teng (1996), performance risk arises from a failure to achieve strategic objectives of partners by partners in an offshore outsourcing relationship despite there being cooperation. Performance risk includes factors related to performance that can lead to a reduction in the firm's performance or failure of a partnership. These factors include incomplete contractual specifications and the lack of capability on the part of the supplier. This lack of capability on part of the supplier leads to reduced quality, delayed delivery, and longer lead time period (Barthelemy, 2003; Herath & Kishore, 2009). Barthelemy (2003) added that the outsourcing firm can make a wrong choice for having little choices or experience to make choices. The shortage of specialized suppliers causes a market shortage. Market shortages escalate costs and creates challenges for firms to benchmark outsourcing performance (Ellram et al., 2008).

Das and Teng (1996) described relational risk as the consequence of partners in inter-firm partnership fail to fully commit to the joint goal. Das and Teng further opined that the success of supplier-buyer outsourcing relationships depends on the cooperation between the two partners involved. Das and Teng noted failure of one partner in an outsourcing relationship to cooperate can lead to reduced confidence in the working relationship, and this could lead to increased perceived relational risk. Williamson (2008) indicated that outsourcing firms often seek to maximize their own gains and other self-interested benefits. Barthelemy (2003) noted outsourcing exchange firms often display opportunistic behaviors, considered the source of relational risks, identified as secretly misusing a partner's knowledge and skills, unbalanced information, miscommunication, and firms' inexperience. Barthelemy stated that these risks could lead to the termination of relationships and the loss of suppliers by the offshoring firm. Das and Teng opined that perceived relational risk is related to trust existing between the offshoring firm and the supplier.

MacAllister (1995) further reinforced the view by Das and Teng (1996) by identifying two forms of trust in an offshore outsourcing relationship: affect-based trust and cognition-based trust. MacAllister noted cognition-based trust arises from achievements arising from direct interactions between the contracting firms. Cognition-based trust can also emerge from the knowledge of performance by partners in an offshore outsourcing engagement. For Ring and Van de Ven (1994), cognitive trust is a calculated risk based on the accumulated knowledge of performance in previous deals. On the contrary, affect-based trust as described by MacAllister establishes on emotional and social bonds between partners in offshoring outsourcing relationship that extends beyond normal business relationship. In this way, this affect-based trust can affect normal business relationship for partners engaged in offshore outsourcing.

The Psychology Perspective: Offshoring Outsourcing Risks

Various studies that approached offshoring from the psychology perspective indicated the offshoring experience poses multiple risks to the staff and the concerned company (Morgan, 2009; Morgan & Symon, 2006). Morgan (2009) noted the offshoring decision could make the staff placed at headquarter of the company feel angry, let down, have a feeling of lack of control, and be uncertain about the future. Morgan further added that the staff of the offshoring company may also feel like the company does not value them or understand their experiences.

Morgan and Symon (2006) argued the transferred staff often remain in contact with the old business entity making it difficult for them to *move-on*. Morgan and Symon further advanced that many individuals affected by outsourcing decision tend to experience the feeling of lack of control. Morgan and Symon argued that for many people, the outsourcing transfer marks the start of other future employment changes. The argument is that outsourcing transfers are often associated with contracts spanning several years and that during these long-term contracts, the employer can make changes at any stage of the negotiation. Similarly, Morgan

(2009) advanced that outsourcing can make the staff feel the previous employer treated them badly and be anxious about future changes. Morgan opined that this happens whenever the outsourcing company's changes their work patterns to control costs. These changes could mean deviating from the previous employer's pattern of working.

A study on downsizing by Allen, Freeman, Russell, Reizestein, and Rentz (2001) indicated that individuals who retain their jobs during offshoring tend to experience *survivor syndrome*. Allen et al. advances that individuals tend to experience a mix of guilt and anxiety because of favorability by the company. Allen et al. further argued that in an outsourcing arrangement, staff retained in the original business entity fits the classic description of *survivor*. According to Allen et al., the transferred staff also fits the survivor description because they survive actual downsizing. The argument is that the transferred staff often experience emotions that are almost like those experienced by staff that lost their jobs. The transferred staff may feel envious of the staff retained in the original company with the consolation that they are not jobless.

There are individual different responses to situations. Although some people may transition with little anxiety, others do not experience strong attachment to the outgoing organization. Still, other individuals may feel attached to their profession and prefer working in an organization that focuses on efficiency and making employees feel valued. Evidence indicated that some organizations achieve substantial improvements in outsourcing contracts, and this could create a good working environment for employees. These and other arguments presented herein suggest that outsourcing or offshoring activities are associated with various psychological risks. These psychological risks are largely associated with the ongoing multiple relationships and transfers of employees. Few studies included discussion about these psychological risks, yet many psychology theories recognize them: exchange theory; identity theory, theories of organizational identification and commitment; attachment theory.

Stress and Coping

Sverke, Hellgren, and Näswall (2002) recognized that one of the stressors experienced by employees during outsourcing transfers is job insecurity. Sverke et al. advanced that job insecurity can adversely affect people involved in outsourcing transfers. Kinunen et al. (2000) reinforces the view that if outsourcing does not provide an opportunity to an individual to develop coping mechanisms, outsourcing could be perceived as unfair and lead to ill health. Fineman (2003) argued that people may view outsourcing as an involuntary transition and a threat to their sense of control, and this could make them to lose the sense of belonging and meaning. Fineman noted outsourcing may influence people to spend their effort gossiping and politicking an attempt to change an unpredictable into a predictable one. This outcome may lead to emotional contagion and charge. Hallier (2000) holds the view that outsourcing could make the staff to hold security in abeyance as they experience the lack of clarity and uncertainty in the change process. After contract violation by the company, employees could have their view shifted towards a view that their relationship with the company and job is more of a transaction. The result of this change in the perspective may be losing the fundamental reason for work, which could lead to long-term problems. The organizational change may have an emotional aspect, which to a certain extent influences how people become concerned about changes in their roles and job loss, as well as the extent of their psychological attachment to the organization.

Attachment Theory

Individual need for attachment may influence the relationships between individuals and their organization and colleagues. As suggested by Feeney and Noller (1996) and Bowlby (1969), the construct of exploration is functionally like work and that employees consider attachment function at work as a secure base. Feeney and Noller noted conditions of chronic and acute stress activate attachment behavior in adults. Outsourcing and other major organizational change may influence attachment behavior in individuals. Feeney and Noller argued several ways exist via which outsourcing may affect an individual. One way is how others respond to the change in the work situation. Kahn (1998) also believed that people need anchoring relationships while at the workplace (i.e., a secure base). Thus, colleagues can support each other in times of crisis by creating a pace for relational work. For Kahn, the outsourcing process may strengthen or break these relational systems.

Identification

Managers use the theories of organizational identification and commitment in work psychology to provide an understanding of individual attachment to organizations as related to outsourcing (Klein, Becker, & Meyer, 2009; Van Knippenberg & van Schie, 2000). As indicated by Klein et al. (2009), in outsourcing, companies often break up groups of people by outsourcing them from different companies. Klein et al. further indicated that the outsourced people may experience disruptions to their workgroup making them upset. Van Knippenberg and van Schie (2000) supported this view by indicating that in professional level outsourcing, employees tend to be remote from their new employer. Sometimes, these new employer moves employees to dedicated offices away from the previous employer. This physical separation of the staff from their previous employer may cause a strain on affective attachment and ultimately lead to detachment. The outsourcing may also impact on an employee's relationships with their new employer (Van Knippenberg & van Schie, 2000).

As reflected in identity theory, some individuals develop pride in an organization or join because of the company's identity. Outsourcing could lead to an employee's transfer to another organization that they had little information about, they have never heard of, or did not choose to work for the organization. Transferred employees may feel ostracized and could lead to difficulties with decision making or problems identifying with the new organization. Studies indicated that perceived organizational identity could impact the out-group and in-group processes, as well as on an individual's sense of self (Albert & Whetton, 1985; Hirschfeld & Field, 2000). As suggested by Hirschfeld and Field (2000), a staff who feel powerless, experience difficult in identifying with the organization, and perceive itself as having little meaning can alienate itself from work.

Exchange Theory

Managers use the exchange theory within the context of work motivation to refer to outsourcing or something else that can be influenced by a change. Exchange theory is crucial in understanding psychological contracts, which synonymous with outsourcing. The theory provides an understanding of how people respond to change. In view of exchange theorists, a psychological contract covers how individuals want other people to treat them and that the psychological contract supplements formal contract between two parties involved in an employment contract (Rousseau, 1995). Studies indicated a relationship between perceived violation of the psychological contract and reduced performance, trust, citizenship behavior, trust, and commitment (Coyle-Shapiro & Kessler, 2002). This violation of the psychological staff identifies as one of the risks of the offshore outsourcing contract. As advanced by Coyle-Shapiro and Kessler (2002), most staff involved in outsourcing feel that the firm that engages in outsourcing transfer often violate their psychological contract. In this way, this contract could potentially create difficult relationships between employees' future and older employers (Coyle-Shapiro & Kessler, 2002). This establishment of short-term limited-security relationships and psychological contract arguably violates employees' need for affiliation and connectedness.

Justice

Fairness or organizational justice is another crucial concept when it comes to outsourcing. Three forms of justice perceptions exist as documented in the extant literature: distributive justice, procedural justice, and interactional justice (Byrne & Cropanzano, 2001). Interactional justice focuses on how the interpersonal treatment offered (i.e., respect, dignity, and sensitivity) perceives as fair or unfair. Procedural justice identifies as procedures used, including control of the process, participation, and decision criteria. Distributive justice focuses on the perceptions of fairness, equality or equity of the outcomes. During outsourcing, justice perceptions tend to be negative because managers often impose change based on one-way communication. Managers feel stressed due to the uncertainty surrounding outsourcing transition. Managers respond to mounting pressure from staff whom they assume have been handed over to another organization and thus no longer their responsibility or problem. As a result, organizational leaders rarely apply fair justice during outsourcing. Fair justice increases the emotional turmoil and stress from the employees.

Outsourcing vs. Offshoring: Business and Psychology Perspectives

Companies have used global offshoring phenomenon since the 1950s. The first wave of offshoring took place post-World War II. During this phase, companies held onto their core functions and aspects of the production activities that gave the firm identity. Companies outsourced labor-intensive operations to offshore facilities abroad. The emergence of internet technologies marked an important milestone in the offshoring realm as the internet facilitated firms to eliminate the physical distance barrier allowing them to outsource new product manufacturing and development to suppliers across the globe. To gain access to ideas and talents from foreign business partners and reduce costs, company leaders started engaging in outsourcing production globally. This phenomenon also influenced firms to relocate high-value functions, including engineering, R & D and design functions abroad. In this way, many companies in different industries in developed economies started outsourcing their production abroad to their offshore facilities.

From the business perspective, drivers or motivators of offshoring as approached from different theoretical perspectives are efficiency (cost reduction); exploitation (developing foreign markets); and exploration (access to talented and knowledge people). From the empirical perspective, drivers of offshoring categorize as: ownership advantages, location advantages, and externalization advantages. Ownership drivers are technological capabilities and resources and international experience in other countries. Location-specific drivers include efficiency-seeking and capability-seeking drivers. Externalizations drivers to offshoring include technological uncertainty and tacit knowledge drivers. Other drivers of offshoring identify as a company seeking to gain core competencies, cost reduction, opportunity to gain relevant specialized knowledge and skills, flexibility from external suppliers, and competitive pressure. Leaders of these companies motivate various factors to engage in offshoring.

The motivational factors group into two categories: horizontal motives (better market access) and vertical motive (lower production costs). The horizontal motive seems to have more traction than vertical motive, especially where high trade barriers exist. However, the vertical motive may be more appealing when trade barriers decline. Companies favor horizontal relocation seeking to jump high trade barriers in order to access markets in other markets. High trade barriers may serve as a hindrance to global fragmentation of production. Although both vertical and horizontal motives involve a certain level of relocating jobs between foreign production and domestic production sites, the term *offshoring* as used within the realm of the public debate typically denotes the relocation of intermediate stages of supply value chain abroad with the goal of serving domestic customers. The idea behind this concept is that by lowering trade barriers, offshoring promotes more vertical relocation than horizontal relocation. In this sense, companies tend to readily understand horizontal relocation as a necessary experience worth undergoing in order to achieve the goal of penetrating foreign markets. In contrast, as long customers are domestic, critics of offshoring are more likely to see vertical relocation as opportunistic behavior to the disadvantage of domestic suppliers and workers.

From the psychology perspective, drivers of offshoring include costs and personal benefits such as possible loss or gain of attractive jobs / tasks by an organization. As demonstrated in this study, companies justify making an offshoring decision as offshoring facilitates the relocation of production abroad facilitating the trade in intermediate services and goods across borders. Evidence from the sectorial studies and firm-level studies indicated that offshoring has a limited negative impact on sector-level employment rather it benefits the domestic labor market. However, worth noting is that the effect of offshoring on domestic employment appears to be more complicated than using foreign workers as a replacement of domestic ones. The wider view and most common view on the effects of offshoring is that offshoring allows firms to tap into cheap foreign employment and thus harming domestic workers. However, while offshoring production may have a direct displace impact on domestic workers, offshoring may have an indirect effect on raising the demand for domestic workers through facilitating the increasing in overall production.

Evidence from the extant literature also indicated that offshoring can enhance productivity by (a) accompanying restructuring measures which minimize inefficiencies; (b) lead to a static efficiency gain; (c) facilitates interactions between internal and foreign suppliers allowing firms to benefit from learning externalities; (d) raise profits and lower the marginal production costs of developing and low-wage countries may and create resources for investing in R & D; and (e) induce selection effects and tougher competition in the markets as well as general equilibrium effects.

From the labor market perspective, offshoring induces cost savings and facilitates an increase in the firm's market share globally and competitiveness. Offshoring also impacts on firm's technology and innovation as R & D offshoring impacts on productivity at home by reallocating market shares and allowing firms to sell more, and that firms achieve this goal by adapting products or services to local needs and charging lower prices. R & D offshoring alters the type of inputs and the nature of the task performed in the home country. Offshoring may serve to argument innovation at the multinational firm's home country by enabling the firm to benefit from the transfer of technology and knowledge from affiliates in the foreign country back home.

In view of these findings, firms justify relocation of production to foreign countries to reduce production costs and gain access to foreign markets. Relocation to foreign markets may also be associated with the destruction in the domestic job; however, the net effect is quite limited and accompanied with task upgrading. The upgrading of the task requires firms to employ domestic workers that have the right skills. A negligible net effect could be concealing wage polarization and non-negligible polarization among domestic workers of varied skills. Therefore, the policy challenge should be to facilitate domestic workers to seize and use the opportunity for job upgrading. The idea of facilitating domestic workers to seize and use the opportunity for job upgrade can be achieved by firms establishing the type of cognitive and communication skills that domestic enterprises find it hard to find abroad. Project managers need to know when outsourcing and offshoring should be used as a solution to a business problem to integrate the most effective strategy going forward. The project manager who knows how to manage remote resources located offshore may provide a critical and needed business skills, particularly in changing times.

In addition, in view of the studies analyzed herein, offshoring is a justifiable means to achieve competitive advantage. Offshoring serves as a useful tool for a company to achieve productivity and cost-saving, and reorganization. No evidence exists to confirm the view that offshoring can be a threat to the economies of advanced countries or a threat to long-term competitiveness and innovative capacities of advanced countries. However, companies choosing to engage in offshoring needs to approach is with caution as there are mitigating risks to achieve the positive impacts highlighted here.

As demonstrated in this book, offshore outsourcing risks are reduced product quality, loss of control over suppliers, and undesirable consequences. From the supply chain business perspective, risks of offshore identify at phase 1 and phase 2 of the outsourcing process Risks at ex-ante contract phase occur during contract development, decision-making, and supplier selection stages of the outsourcing process. During this phase, notable risks are supply market environment risks, namely economic risks, cultural risks, and political risks. Others include political risks, environmental regulations and laws, unpredictable changes in labor, political instability, language and cultural barriers. Risks during the ex-post contract phase occur during supplier management stage of the offshore outsourcing process. These risks include experience risks; opportunistic behaviors and insufficient capability on the part of the supplier; firm's lack of experience in offshore outsourcing; risks of escalating costs linked to unexpected management costs and transactions; risks related to outsourcing expertise and experience and internal uncertainty in relation to outsourcing requirements, risks associated with supplier's opportunistic behaviors; and lack of capability; and unintentional knowledge leakage and conflicts. Company leaders must also be prepared to mitigate performance and relational risks when considering offshoring. Performance risk arises from a failure to achieve strategic objectives of partners by partners in an offshore outsourcing relationship despite there being cooperation. Performance risk includes factors related to performance that can lead to a reduction in the firm's performance or failure of a partnership. These factors include incomplete contractual specifications and the lack of capability on the part of the supplier.

The result of the analysis of studies on re-shoring also suggests that the critics of offshoring may be wrong on drivers of re-shoring. In view of the findings analyzed herein, various factors influenced companies to reconsider their offshoring decisions in favor of re-shoring. Notable drivers of re-shoring include cost concerns; lack of internal competence; quality concerns; location factors (the growth of regional and local market (i.e., wage costs); human capital; the availability of resources;

scientific infrastructure; and the presence of suppliers). Other location factors known to drive re-shoring include underestimation and miscalculation of full costs; production, innovation and co-location of R & D; offshoring as a potential threat to intellectual property; balancing risk dispersion and costs savings; proximity to the market to achieve flexibility; and the oil/shale gas resolution in the United States and a weakening dollar. Some companies do not recognize the intended consequences of offshoring activities. Failure to recognize the risks of offshoring have led to the failure by companies to achieve the intended objectives of offshoring. Unfortunately, the companies now consider re-shoring production back to home countries or those closer to the respective parent countries.

In view of these findings, it is worth concluding that companies should continue the re-shoring practices for reasons discussed herein. While various forms of trade barriers, notably legal, informational, and administrative barriers exist, offshoring may be a worthy decision as it may be the most effective way to reach foreign customers. Relocating production abroad may also be an effective way to source from cheap foreign suppliers and thus cut costs. Companies can also capitalize on offshoring to directly seek low wage labor abroad.

THOUGHTS FROM THE ACADEMIC ENTREPRENEUR

The Problem to be Solved:

- Project Managers' ineffective using BPO and offshoring services to augment project staff or services.

The Goals:

- Understanding the different offshoring models.
- Similarities in costs between offshoring and DIY.
- Help project managers select competent groups to aid in offshoring services.

The Questions to Ask:

- How can organizations effectively prepare to use offshore and BPO services?
- Can cultural issues be overcome when implementing offshoring staff?

Today's Business Application:

- Effective leaders who understand domestic and international cultures and know how to be effective despite differences are better equipped to respond successfully to business problems.
- Preparation is fundamental to prevent or lessen the effects of mismanaging offshore staff.
- Continuous communication inside and outside the organization will help leaders and project management teams resolve the cultural gaps and lessen conflicts.

REFERENCES

Albert, S., & Whetten, D. A. (1985). Organizational identity. *Research in Organizational Behaviour, 7,* 263–295. Retrieved from https://psycnet.apa.org/record/1986-02640-001

Allen, T. D., Freeman, D. M., Russell, J. E., Reizestein, R. C., & Rentz, J. O. (2001). Survivor reactions to organizational downsizing: Does time ease the pain? *Journal of Occupational and Organizational Psychology, 74*(2), 145-164. doi:10.1348/096317901167299

Aron, R., & Singh, J. (2005). Getting offshoring right. *Harvard Business Review, 83,* 135-147. Retrieved from http://hbr.org/2005/12/getting-offshoring-right/ar/1

Bahli, B., & Rivard, S. (2003). The information technology outsourcing risk: A transaction cost and agency theory-based perspective. *Journal of Information Technology, 18*(3), 211-221. Retrieved from https://www.tandfonline.com/toc/rjit20/18/3?nav=tocList

Barthelemy, J. (2003). The seven deadly sins of outsourcing. *Academy of Management Executive, 17*(2), 87-98. doi:10.5465/AME.2003.10025203

Bowlby, J. (1969). *Attachment and loss: Attachment.* New York, NY: Basic Books.

Byrne, Z. S., & Cropanzano, R. (2001). History of organizational justice: The founders speak. In R. Cropanzano (Ed.), *Justice in the workplace. Vol. II: From theory to practice.* Mahwah, NJ: Lawrence Erlbaum.

Cavusgil, S. T., Yaprak, A., &Yeoh, P. (1993). A decision-making framework for global sourcing. *International Business Review, 2*(2), 143-156. doi:10.1016/0969-5931(93)90011-K

Costa, C. (2001). Information technology outsourcing in Australia: A literature review. *Information Management and Computer Security, 9*(5), 213-224. doi:10.1108/EUM0000000006068

Coyle-Shapiro, J. A. M., & Kessler, I. (2002). Exploring reciprocity through the lens of the psychological contract: Employee and employer perspectives. *European Journal of Work and Organizational Psychology, 11*(1), 69–86. doi:10.1080/13594320143000852

Das, T. K., & Teng, B. (1996). Risk types and inter-firm alliance structures. *Journal of Management Studies, 33,* 827-843. doi:10.1111/j.1467-6486.1996.tb00174.x

Demirbag, M., Mellahi, S., Sahadev, K., & Elliston, J. (2012). Employee service abandonment in service operations: A case study of a US multinational in India. *Journal of World Business, 47*(2), 178-185. doi:10.1016/j.jwb.2011.04.004

Dhar, S., & Balakrishnan, B. (2006). Risks, benefits, and challenges in global IT outsourcing: Perspectives and practices. *Journal of Global Information Management, 14*(3), 59-89. doi:10.4018/jgim.2006070104

Earl, M. J. (1996). The risks of outsourcing IT. *Sloan Management Review, 37*(3), 26-32. doi:10.4236/ib.2013.53B036

Ellram, L. M., Tate, W. L., & Billington, C. (2008). Offshore outsourcing of professional services: A transaction cost economics perspective. *Journal of Operations Management, 26*(2), 148-163. doi:10.1016/j.jom.2007.02.008

Enderwick, P. (2008). Quality assurance and upgrading in global supply chains: Implications for management in a transition economy. *Thunderbird International Business Review, 50*(4), 217-230. doi:10.1002/tie.20200

Feeney, J., & Noller, P. (1996). *Adult attachment*. Thousand Oaks, CA: Sage.

Fineman, S. (2003). *Understanding emotions at work*. London, UK: Sage.

Freeman, R. (2005). What really ails Europe (and America): The doubling of the global workforce. *The Globalist*. Retrieved from http://www.theglobalist.com

Ghoshal, S., (1987). Global strategy: An organizing framework. *Strategic Management Journal., 8*, 425-440. doi:10.1002/smj.4250080503

Graf, M., & Mudambi S. M. (2005). The outsourcing of IT-enabled business processes: A conceptual model of the location decision. *Journal of International Management, 11*(2), 253-268. doi:10.1016/j.intman.2005.03.010

Hallier, J. (2000). Security abeyance: Coping with the erosion of job conditions and treatment. *British Journal of Management, 11*(1),71–89. doi:10.1111/1467-8551.00152

Haried, P., & Ramamurthy, K. (2009). Evaluating the success in international sourcing of information technology projects: The need for a relational client-vendor approach. *Project Management Journal, 40*(3), 56-71. doi:10.1002/pmj.20113

Herath, T., & Kishore, R. (2009). Offshore outsourcing: Risks, challenges, and potential solutions. *Information Systems Management, 26*(4), 312-326. doi:10.1080/10580530903245549

Hirschfeld, R. R., & Field, H. S. (2000). Work centrality and work alienation: Distinct aspects of a general commitment to work. *Journal of Organizational Behaviour, 21*, 789–800. doi:10.1002/1099-1379(200011)21:73.0.CO;2-W

Kahn, W. A. (1998). Relational systems at work. *Research in Organizational Behaviour, 20*, 39–76. doi:10.5465/amr.2011.0363

Kakumanu, P., & Portanova, A. (2006). Outsourcing: Its benefits, drawbacks, and other related issues. *Journal of American Academy of Business, 9*(2), 1-7. Retrieved from http://www.jaabc.com/jaabcv9n2preview.html

Klein, H. J., Becker, T. E., & Meyer, J. P. (2009). *Commitment in organizations (SIOP Organizational Frontiers Series)*. New York, NY: Routledge.

Kotabe, M., & Murray, J. (2004). Global sourcing strategy and sustainable competitive advantage. *Industrial Marketing Management, 33*(1). 7-14. doi 10.1016/j.indmarman.2003.08.004

Lee, J., & Kim, Y. (1999). Effect of partnership quality on IS outsourcing success: Conceptual framework and empirical validation. *Journal of Management Information Systems, 15*(4), 29-61. doi:10.1080/07421222.1999.11518221

Li, X., & Barnes, I. (2008). Proactive supply risk management methods for building a robust supply selection process when sourcing from emerging markets. *Strategic Outsourcing: An International Journal, 1*(3), 252-267. doi:10.1108/17538290810915308

Mahnke, V., Lucas, M., & Vang, J. (2005). Strategic outsourcing of IT services: Theoretical stocktaking and empirical challenges. *Industry and Innovation, 12*(2), 205-253. doi:10.1080/13662710500087958

Manning, S., Massini, S., & Lewin, C. (2008). A dynamic perspective on next-generation offshoring: The global sourcing of science and engineering talent. *Academy of Management Perspectives, 20*(3), 35-54. doi:10.5465/AMP.2008.34587994

Mcallister, D. (1995). Affect-and cognition based trust as foundations for interpersonal cooperation in organizations. *Academy of Management Journal, 38*(1), 24-59. doi:10.5465/256727

McIvor, R. (2009). How the transaction cost and resource-based theories of the firm inform outsourcing evaluation. *Journal of Operations Management, 27,* 45-63. doi 10.1016/j.jom.2008.03.004

Mohr, J., & Spekman, R. (1994). Characteristics of partnership success: Partnership attributes, communication behavior, and conflict resolution techniques. *Strategic Management Journal, 15*(2), 135-152. doi:10.1002/smj.4250150205

Morgan, R. M., & Hunt, S. D. (1994). The commitment-trust theory of relationship marketing. *Journal of Marketing, 58*(3), 20–38. doi:10.1177/002224299405800302

Morgan, S. J., & Symon, G. (2006). The experience of outsourcing transfer: Implications for guidance and counselling. *British Journal of Guidance and Counselling, 34*(2), 191-207. doi:10.1080/03069880600583238

Morgan, S. J. (2009). *The human side of outsourcing: Psychological theory and management practice.* Oxford, UK: Wiley-Blackwell.

Morgan, S. J., & Symon, G. (2006). The experience of outsourcing transfer: Implications for guidance and counselling. *British Journal of Guidance and Counselling, 34*(2), 191-207. doi:10.1080/03069880600583238

Norwood, J., Carson, C., Deese, N., Johnson, F, Reader, J., & Schwab, S. (2006). Off-shoring: An elusive phenomenon. *National Academy of Public Administration.* A Report of the Panel of the National Academy of Public Administration for the U.S. Congress and the Bureau of Economic Analysis.

Palugod, N. (2011). Global trends in offshoring and outsourcing. *International Journal of Business and Social Science*, 2(16), 11-19. Retrieved from http://ijbssnet.com/journals/Vol_2_No_16_September_2011/2.pdf

Quinn, J. B., & Hilmer, F. G. (1994). Strategic outsourcing. *Sloan Management Review*, 35(4), 43-55. Retrieved from https://sloanreview.mit.edu/article/strategic-outsourcing/

Ring, P. S., & Van de Ven, A. H. (1994). Developmental processes of cooperative inter-organizational relationships. *Academy of Management Review*, 19, 90-118. doi:10.2307/258836

Rousseau, D. M. (1995). *Psychological contracts in organizations: Understanding written and unwritten agreements*. Thousand Oaks, CA: Sage.

Salaberrios, I. (2020, March). *Outsourcing vs. offshoring: Business and psychology perspectives*. Grayslake, IL: Pensiero Press. *Excerpts reprinted with permission.

Schniederjans, M., & Zuckweiler, K. (2004), A quantitative approach to the outsourcing-insourcing decision in an international context. *Management Decision*, 42, 974-986. doi:10.1108/00251740410555461

Sethupathy, G. (2013, August). Offshoring, wages, and employment: Theory and evidence. *European Economic Review*, 62, 73-97 https://dx.doi.org/10.1016/j.euroecorev.2013.04.004

Stehrer, R., Borowiecki, M., Dachs, B., Hanzl-Weiss, D., Kinkel, S., Pöschl, J., Sass, M., Schmall, T. C., & Szalavetz, A. (2012). Global value chains and the EU industry. *WIIW Research Reports no. 383*, Vienna.

Sverke, M., Hellgren, J., & Näswall, K. (2002). No security: A meta-analysis and review of job insecurity and its consequences. *Journal of Occupational Health Psychology*, 7, 242–252. doi:10.1037/1076-8998.7.3.242

Van Knippenberg, D., & van Schie, E. C. M. (2000). Foci and correlates of organizational identification. *Journal of Occupational and Organizational Psychology*, 73(2), 137–148. doi:10.1348/096317900166949

Willcocks, L., Hindle, J., Feeny, D., & Lacity, M. (2004) IT and business process outsourcing: The knowledge potential. *Information System Management*, 21(3), 7-15. doi:10.1201/1078/44432.21.3.20040601/82471.2

Williamson, O. E. (2008), Outsourcing: Transaction cost economics and supply chain management*. *Journal of Supply Chain Management*, 44, 5-16. doi:10.1111/j.1745-493X.2008.00051.x

About the Author...

Dr. Ivan Salaberrios resides in Pickerington, Ohio. Dr. Ivan holds several accredited degrees; a Bachelor of Technical management Science (BS) in Management from DeVry University; a Master of Business Administration (MBA) from Keller Graduate School; and a Doctor of Business Administration (DBA) from Walden University. Dr. Ivan also is a certified Project Management Professional (PMP) and Lean Six Sigma Black Belt Certified

Dr. Ivan is the CEO and founder of AIM Technical Consultants. His career in the telecommunications industry began as a field engineer working with AMPs Radio Equipment, where he obtained extensive experience in RF Engineering, Network Engineering and Project Management.

In 20 years, Dr. Ivan has grown AIM from a handful of engineers to one of the largest staffing and engineering firms focused exclusively in wireless telecom. This growth is largely attributable to Ivan's relationship-building skills, dedication to exceptional service delivery, and unwavering focus on continuous improvement. Dr. Ivan is a Gulf War veteran, serving an enlistment term in the U.S. Navy on the USS *Yorktown* CG-48. He was honorably discharged in 1992.

To reach Dr. Ivan Salaberrios for information on consulting, please **e-mail: ivans@aimtechinc.com**

About the Company...

AIM Technical Consultants has experienced significant wireless industry growth since opening for business in 1999. We attribute this proven track record to our ability to consistently deliver IT field management and wireless technology implementation, allowing our customers peace of mind. Add to that our dedication to providing the best technical and professional services in the industry and AIM Technical Consultant's commitment to positioning ourselves as the *go to* wireless industry service provider, and the results speak for themselves. AIM Technical provides services in IT and wireless telecommunications committed to delivering unparalleled Cloud Engineering life-cycle support to our demanding customers with specific IT and wireless telecommunication needs.

For more information, please contact **email: office@aimtechnical.com, phone: 614-866-1472**, website: https://www.aimtechnical.com/

CHAPTER 6

Care Coordination Models in Accountable Care Organizations: Achievements, Challenges, and Opportunities

Dr. Alla Adams

Accountable care organization (ACO) models were created in 2012 to enhance population health, improve patient care, and reduce costs. ACOs are groups of independent health care providers that implement a transformation in the way health care is organized across the continuum. Creating such a group is a project that involves identifying and aligning thinking alike providers, creating an ACO, transforming how each ACO member entity operates, converting each provider to a quality driven organization, while effectively managing financial risk. This process requires expertise in project management to be successful. Recent literature highlights the achievements ACOs have reported in improving quality and lowering costs, as well as the challenges these organization have experienced. The shift from volume to value, or from fee-for-service to value-based reimbursement, represents a cultural change that the ACOs are challenged to make to succeed in the current financial climate.

Care Coordination Models in Accountable Care Organizations: Achievements, Challenges, and Opportunities

To fulfill an important aspect of better care coordination and increasing value of health care services, the Patient Protection and Affordable Care Act (ACA) encouraged health care providers to engage in networks that incentivize them to deliver care more efficiently and provide affordable, quality health care services. ACA introduced new care coordination models in the forms of Centers of Medicare and Medicaid Services (CMS) demonstrations, pilots, and programs focused on quality and patient-centeredness. The Institute for Health Improvement (2020) introduced the Triple Aim framework that describes an approach to optimizing health system performance and includes three concepts of improving the patient experience of care, improving population health, and reducing the per capital cost of health care. Further, with the move toward delivering a value-based and more comprehensive care, the concept or Triple Aim shifted toward the Quadruple Aim that includes promoting the well-being of health care services providers (Bohenheimer & Sinsky, 2014).

Along with the increasing push for imparting value-based care, several relatively new care models such as Accountable Care Organizations (ACOs), Patient-Centers Medical Homes (PCMHs), and Consumer Operated and Oriented Plans (CO-OPs) have come to existence. Each model has been demonstrating great achievements, experiencing unique challenges, and offering new opportunities. Project management approaches have been essential in helping to achieve these models' many benefits, including better control of resources, decreasing costs, improving care coordination, and quality of care.

Accountable Care Organizations

ACOs are networks of independent health care providers who partner together to provide high-quality, coordinated care to the Medicare patients they serve. This model goal is to avoid unnecessary medical errors and duplication of services. ACOs' ideal successful outcome is that patients would have higher quality of care with minimum procedures or tests, reducing cost and utilization; better outcomes would lower Medicare spending and reduce the tax burden; and when high value care is delivered and dollars spend more wisely, the participants will share the savings they achieved for the Medicare program. The success of an ACO depends on its organized effort to keep the patient population as healthy as possible and to mitigate chronic disease. This model encourages improving preventative care, which in time should provide better outcomes for the given amount of cost within covered population. Seven types of ACOs have been established so far: Medicare Shared Savings Program, the Investment Model, Advance Payment ACO Model, Comprehensive ESRD Care Initiative (for dialysis services), Pioneer ACO Model, Vermont All-Payer ACO Model, and Next Generation ACO Model.

ACO Types

Medicare Shared Savings Program (MSSP) is an initial ACO model established by the ACA for coordinating care and implementing population health management approaches for Medicare Fee For Service (FFS) beneficiaries. This model requires that all aspects of a patient's preventive and chronic care be guided through a longitudinal relationship with a primary care physician who helps to navigate the system and access specialty services as needed. Under this model, there is shared responsibility for cost of care not only by physicians in the ACO, but also the care of the physicians outside of the ACO. This model has different tracks that allow the provider group to select an arrangement that appears to work best for their organization. Unlike the bundled payment reimbursement model, the ACO does not have a finite time limit and the provider is expected to manage both preventive and chronic conditions. CMS sets specific savings target and if target is missed may demand some of the previously paid money back. If target is met, health care services quality is evaluated. If quality is poor, providers will not receive any additional bonus payment. If quality is good, bonus is paid, sharing the savings between the participating providers. A combination of savings and quality considerations determine whether bonus is big or small. As of the beginning of 2020, 517 ACOs participate in this model, providing care to 11.2 million beneficiaries (Centers of Medicare and Medicaid Services, 2020a).

The Investment Model is used when some providers lack sufficient funds needed to invest in infrastructure necessary to successfully implement population health management approaches. Medicare provides financial support to the ACO and so in a way provides pre-paid shared savings. ACO receives pre-payment from Medicare and uses it to invest in infrastructure to implement new ways to improve patient care coordination. This model was introduced in 2015, is still ongoing, and as of the beginning of 2020, includes 45 participating ACOs (Centers of Medicare and Medicaid Services, 2020b).

Advance Payment ACO Model provides advance, up-front payment to ACOs in MSSP model. It works for certain eligible rural and physician-owned organizations already in or interested in the MSSP, whose ability to achieve the triple aim would be improved with access to additional capital. Participants receive monthly payments upfront from Medicare and use the money to make investments in their care coordination infrastructure. This model was introduced in 2012, it included 35 participating

ACOs, and it is no longer active (Centers of Medicare and Medicaid Services, 2020c).

Comprehensive End-Stage Renal Disease (ESRD) Care Initiative is the first disease-specific ACO model designed for Medicare beneficiaries with ESRD receiving dialysis services. Medicare partners with suppliers and health care providers to test the effectiveness of new service model that provides beneficiaries with high quality, person-centered care. This model was introduced in 2017, and as of the beginning of 2020 has 33 participating ACOs (Centers of Medicare and Medicaid Services, 2020d).

Pioneer ACO Model was used by providers and health care organizations already experienced in coordinating patient care. This model allowed rapid move from savings to population-based payment models. Population-based payment was a per beneficiary per month payment amount intended to replace 50% of the ACO's fee-for-service (FFS) payment with prospective payment. This model was more advanced and flexible than MSSP. It was introduced in 2012 and concluded in December 2016 with 9 ACOs participating (Centers of Medicare and Medicaid Services, 2020e).

Vermont All-Payer ACO Model is an Advanced Alternative Payment Model for the state of Vermont. In this model, the most significant payers throughout the entire state – Medicare, Medicaid, and commercial health care payers – incentivize health care value and quality, with a focus on health outcomes, under the same payment structure for the ACOs in Vermont. Under the Vermont model, the state commits to achieves statewide financial, health outcomes and ACO scale targets throughout all health care payers. This model was announced in 2016, and as of the beginning of 2020 includes one participant that is in the State of Vermont (Centers of Medicare and Medicaid Services, 2020f).

Next Generation ACO Model was launched combining experience from the MSSP and Pioneer ACO Models. This model sets predictable financial targets, allows more flexibility in care coordination, and focuses on attaining the highest quality standards of care. It allows participating providers to assume higher levels of financial risk and higher levels of reward comparing to MSSP. This model was introduced in 2016 and currently includes 41 participants (Centers of Medicare and Medicaid Services, 2020g).

Quality of Care Measures

With such firm financial requirements to decrease costs, the quality of care must be protected. To receive the shared savings reward from Medicare, ACOs must meet quality standards. CMS measure quality of care using 31 nationally recognized quality measures in four areas: patient/caregiver experience (8 measures); care coordination/patient safety (10 measures); clinical care for at-risk population: Diabetes (2 measures scored as one composite measure), Hypertension (1 measure), Ischemic Vascular Disease (1 measure), Depression (1 measure); and preventive health (8 measures). These 31 quality measures are reported and calculated using Medicare claims data (7 measures), Quality Payment Program Advancing Care Information (ACI) data (1 measure), CMS Web Interface ACO-reported clinical quality measure data (15 measures), and patient experience of care survey data (8 measures) (Centers of Medicare and Medicaid Services, 2018). The level of ACO performance on quality measures and demonstrated improvement over time has substantial impact on an ACO's total shared savings rate. Therefore, to be successful and receive the greatest amount of shared savings, ACOs must focus on cutting costs and scoring high on quality measures.

Project Management Within and Beyond a Healthcare Organization

What makes an ACO successful is using project management approaches for coordination. Coordination within each and between independent healthcare organizations is essential because together, they form a complex ACO structure and each member institution shares their specialization, making the overall health care delivery approach less fragmented. These innovative organizations depend on project managers to bring the ACO's goals and plans to life. Project managers work to ensure assigned projects are completed within established constraints of time, budget, scope, and risk. When various independent entities, members of the ACO, must share resources (i.e., staff, equipment, and information), coordination is essential.

Because ACOs are open systems, the member organizations must coordinate their work between each other or in their external environment. Coordination occurs in four directions: (a) vertical (connects work up and down the vertical hierarchy in an organization), (b) horizontally (connects work sideways across an organization), (c) diagonally (simultaneously connects work vertically and horizontally), and (d) externally (connects work with other organizations) (Olden, 2019). How do project managers strengthen coordination for the ACO? Project managers create structures and processes that enable each ACO member organization's employees to exchange information. ACO members redesign their organizations' structure to strengthen horizontal coordination by including interdisciplinary teams and project teams.

This organizational structure redesign involves several critical components. The first component is hierarchical referral (Olden, 2019). It is the chain of command to exchange information up and down a vertical hierarchy. The second component is mutual adjustment (Olden, 2019). Staff who do not have a supervisor-subordinate relationship informally exchange information to coordinate their work. The third component includes rules, plans, and protocols. These create standard outputs and standardized processes (Olden, 2019). For example, a protocol can specify for the primary care team which specialists should be consulted for a new patient with a specific chronic disease diagnosis. The fourth component is information systems (Olden, 2019). Adopting a common or shared electronic information system is critical. It is used for entering, collecting, analyzing, and reporting information within each member organization and between all ACO organizations. Electronic whiteboards, project management software, collaborative document-editing tools, meeting management groupware are especially useful. The electronic information system is also used for periodic reports of key performance indicators to selected physicians, administrative staff, and other stakeholders. The fifth component is project management. A full-time integrator or a project manager devotes their time to coordinating multiple organizations or their units (Olden, 2019). The project manager does not supervise any units or departments, but integrates employees from each of them to coordinate their work toward a common purpose.

Several specific features are critical for the ACO model success—access to primary care, using population health strategies that identify patients who need services for prevention or chronic disease management, and ensuring that patients have a positive experience during provider visits. ACOs are able to adopt technology that small independent facilities cannot afford. They are adopting faster the electronic health records (EHR) system. ACO model allows to track, communicate, and share information across the organization of independent providers through technology interfaces. Providers may require payment prior to providing a service for the reasons of helping to build a foundation for certain ACO and invest in its infrastructure. The model allows to hold doctors and health care providers accountable for their patients' health by pushing providers to improve quality of services. ACOs must measure and report improvements. Also, ACOs must plan and coordinate patient care among the different aspects and settings of the services provided. An effective strategy depends partially on the ACO's ability to engage patients in managing their own care and modifying their health behavior. In contrast to most of traditional episodic care, this approach is continuous. This means that the providers should proactively reach out to patients who needs chronic care or preventive check-ups and bring them in for follow-up.

D'Aunno, Broffman, Sparer, and Kumar (2018) examined claims data from the CMS and data from 60 interviews of three high-performing and three low-performing ACOs and identified that the following factors distinguish high- from low-performing ACOs: "(1) collaboration with hospitals; (2) effective physician group practice prior to ACO engagement; (3) trusted, long-standing physician leaders focused on improving performance; (4) sophisticated use of information systems; (5) effective feedback to physicians; and (6) embedded care coordinators" (p. 120).

A survey of ACOs conducted by McAlearney, Walker, and Hefner (2018) showed that moving from volume to value is vital to the culture change required of an ACO. If before the key to success was full schedule or full census for hospitals, now the key is the healthy outcomes or general well-being of the covered population. The ship is turning around. In contrast to typical physician practices that are concentrating on scheduling individual patients, ACO physicians must focus on the health risks of their entire patient networks. To gather data and statistics, they require their patients to complete a health risk assessment. Unlike the current practice model (or treating sick care model), the ACO model focuses on prevention and its long-term effects by proactive outreach and early identification.

What are the Pros of ACOs?

- The ideal ACO model is for the patients to have a higher quality of care with the minimum procedures or tests
- Reducing cost and utilization
- Ability to harness real-time data from the EHR to categorize patients in their populations and understand more about achieved patient outcomes
- Certain anti-trust protection
- Ability to negotiate collectively with private insurers. Many local markets have high level of insurers' consolidation, making it difficult for providers to negotiate individually
- A successful ACO needs to allow fair compensation to the medical providers to ensure they stay in the program over time
- The most successful ACOs are focused on three areas: (a) high value culture, (b) configuring effective population health management programs, and (c) implementing structures to ensure contiguous performance improvement over time.

Challenges:

- Start-up costs of ACOs for providers are high. Information technology and care coordination in ACOs are complicated and expensive to implement.
- Often ACOs do not have the right stakeholders when setting up the governance structure. All stakeholder requirements need to be addressed or the ACO will fail to integrate. All the providers need is to change the way they provide services. For example, not changing from FFS to integrated care quick enough – the ACO will struggle and may fail.

- Stakeholders underestimate the time it takes to roll out a full functioning ACO. Many roll outs take longer than six months.

- A big mistake is not making information technology a top priority. Everyone in the ACO needs to be on a compatible electronic health care records system, and other applications for smooth interoperability. Most small organizations struggle with it because of high costs.

- Blackstone and Fuhr (2016) indicated that even though providers are incentivized to control health services costs, patients receiving care in ACOs have little incentive to use low-cost quality services and providers. Coordination of care becomes more challenging when patients go to physicians outside of the ACO.

- Lack of data standardization impedes data-driven health care. Madsen (2014) believed that because of health care data complexity, the current state of health care business intelligence does not provide for the industry needs and the failure rate of data warehouses is unfortunately high. Data are asset and they should be managed that way. It sounds like protecting data should be a simple endeavor. "But it's about as difficult as a task can be. It is a lot like trying to prevent a flood where the water will go wherever it wants to go" (Madsen, 2014, p. 93). Frequently, nobody is sure where the data are, who has touched them, and when or why.

- DeCamp, et al. (2014) conducted a structured review of medical literature related to ACOs and using qualitative content analysis identified the following ethical issues:

  > Leaders could face challenges regarding fair resource allocation (e.g., about fairly using ACOs' shared savings), protection of professionals' ethical obligations (especially related to

the design of financial incentives), and development of fair decision processes (e.g., ensuring that beneficiary representatives on the ACO board truly represent the ACO's patients). (p. 1392)

There could be a perceived threat to the clinicians' professional autonomy because of cost control measures and a sense of conflicted responsibility to their patients and the ACO. For patients, ethical challenges may include protecting their autonomy, privacy and confidentiality.

Achievements

In July 2019, the Office of Inspector General of the U.S. Department of Health and Human Services (2019) posted results of a study of 20 high performing MSSP ACOs. The findings showed a number of strategies these ACOs implemented that were found to be successful in reducing Medicare spending and improving quality of care. These strategies included seven categories: "working with physicians, engaging beneficiaries, managing beneficiaries with costly or complex care needs, managing hospitalizations, managing skilled nursing and home health care, addressing behavioral health needs and social determinants of health, and using technology for information sharing" (p. 6). ACOs advise participating physicians in office workflows to help address gaps in care and avoid duplication. ACOs require participating physicians who do not have electronic health record (EHR) system to select and adopt one within 1 year of joining. According to the Office of the National Coordinator for Health Information Technology (2019), 86% of office-based physicians adopted an EHR system as of 2017, which is up from 51% in 2010.

ACOs use annual wellness visits to build relationships between physicians and beneficiaries and to engage beneficiaries in their health. For example, one ACO in the Office of Inspector

General of the U.S. Department of Health and Human Services (2019) study assists participating physicians identify beneficiaries who have not had an annual wellness visit and set up corresponding appointments. The ACO physicians reported an increase of annual wellness visits form 15% to more than 50% in 2017.

The CMS has been implementing alternative payments models, such as MSSP, that reward providers for the value of services as a part of the conscious transition from the fee-for-service to value-based reimbursement. According to a national study of 120 health care payers conducted by ORC International and sponsored by Change Health care (Pennic, 2018), fee-for-service is declining faster than predicted—decreasing from 51.7% of reimbursement in 2016 to 37.2% in 2018, and further projected to decrease to 25.4% by 2021. As a big shift toward the Triple Aim, 77% of payers reported improvements in care quality, 73% reported improved patient engagement, and 64% reported improvement in provider relationships.

National Association of ACOs (2018) conducted comprehensive review of estimates of savings by MSSP ACOs and reported that ACOs saved Medicare $2.66 billion during a period from 2013 to 2016.

Opportunities

Supported by the ACA for Medicare beneficiaries and by commercial health plans, as of the beginning of 2020, there are about 600 ACOs. Each ACO is accountable for the clinical and financial outcomes of its covered population via complex contracts with payers. ACOs are constantly looking for opportunities for improvement to be effective, such as continuous clinical integration initiatives, organizational culture transformation, data integration, and keeping eyes on the brass ring - long-term population health.

There is a growing body of literature that indicates that focuses on the health and well-being of the covered populations, with the rise of the opioid epidemic and increase in suicide rates, there is an opportunity for the ACOs for collaboration with public health and behavioral health organizations to address challenges in mental health and addiction facing their communities (Bommersbach, et al., 2018). Ingram, Scutchfield, and Costich (2015) examined areas of potential collaboration between public health agencies and ACOs and suggested that public health agencies can help ACOs partner with various community organizations, reach vulnerable patients, promote policies that improve member health, and provide population-based services and surveillance data.

Gray and Sheiko (2016) believed that annual performance measurement as conceived under ACO models does not occur frequently enough to provide ACOs actionable insight into areas where improvements are needed. Measurements need to be conducted more than once a year and trended data need to be tracked. Eventually, ACOs will, by necessity, must utilize aspects of navigation and advocacy assistance so that patients access the right care at the right time. Japinga, Alexander, and McClellan (2019) suggested that improving model components, such as quality measurement and risk adjustment, and building a diverse palliative care-trained workforce will accelerate progress by helping more ACOs participate in serious illness models and develop capabilities to improve care. Williams (2016) found that physician led ACOs are usually more flexible than those affiliated with a hospital. Physician-led ACOs can focus more intently on lowering the cost of delivering primary care, implement more effective cost-saving initiatives, and achieve higher shared saving rates.

To support the primary elements of their success, ACOs need to have current and historic electronic data for patient population, certain level of commitment to quality improvement and evidence-based practice, longitudinal relationships with patients to mitigate chronic conditions, and pleasant patient experiences. According to Gensinger (2014), prompts, alerts, and all means of practice direction or decision support can be delivered at a point in time when needed to make a difference in patient outcomes. Both the technology and the data are advancing. The volume, timeliness, and quality of clinical data are exploding, with more structured clinical data anticipated in the near future. Data analytics and business intelligence can also contribute to the growing emphasis on population health management, which requires a broad range of analytics capabilities. As ACOs continue to develop and try to capitalize on economies of scale, their need to optimize processes and services will be essential. The ability to use advanced predictive and prescriptive modeling methods to assist in the optimization efforts can be the difference between success and failure.

Conclusion

One of the change-driving vehicles of the Affordable Care Act are the ACOs. These groups of independent physicians and hospitals share both a medical and financial responsibility for the health of their covered population. Instead of focusing on volume or multiple visits and the corresponding high bills as had previously been the case, ACOs focus on fewer visits, preventive care and well-coordinated, more complete care. Project management approaches for coordination within each and between ACO member organizations have been key to the ACO model success. Through participation in an ACO, independent physician practices gain access to customizable care management services and tools, innovations, and better reimbursement payments. Care historically has been fragmented, but now health care managers can strengthen coordination because of payment changes that reward coordinated care. For ACO providers, operating successfully can lead to financial rewards. For patients, lowering medical bills, decreasing duplication of services, and improving the outcomes should increase the value of the services that they purchase. New ACOs are in for the long haul and are up for change in processes of care, new reporting systems, staff competencies, cultural change, and analytics. ACOs will improve with experience; and the longer they participate in the program, the more likely they will manage costs effectively, improve quality measures, and earn shared savings.

THOUGHTS FROM THE ACADEMIC ENTREPRENEUR

The Problem to be Solved:

- What new care coordination models are emerging in the health care industry shifting from volume to value?

The Goals:

- To define the Accountable Care Organizations (ACOs) types and models
- To understand the achievements and challenges of the ACOs
- To examine the opportunities for ACOs' success in improving the health of the covered population

The Questions to Ask:

- What are the pros of ACOs?
- What are the challenges faced by the ACOs?
- What are the opportunities for overcoming the ACO challenges and improving the health of the covered population?

Today's Business Application:

- Effective care coordination and financial incentives models can provide the necessary foundation for decreasing the health care costs and improving the health care quality.
- The ACOs are still in beta-testing and it is important to examine how their models are evolving.
- The regulatory emphasis on overall population health management could continue to increase the financial accountability pressure on physicians and hospitals to improve health care services outcomes and the health of the covered population.

REFERENCES

Blackstone, E. A., & Fuhr, J. P. (2016). The economics of Medicare accountable care organizations. *American Health and Drug Benefits, 9*(1), 11-19. Retrieved from https://www.ncbi.nlm.nih.gov/pmc/articles/PMC4822974/

Bohenheimer, T., & Sinsky, C. (2014). From triple to quadruple aim: Care of the patient requires care of the provider. *Annals of Family Medicine, 12*, 573-576. doi:10.1370/afm.1713

Bommersbach, T., Borger, K., Steverman, S., Manderscheid, R. W., Sharfstein, J., & Everett, A. (2018). Behavioral health, local Health Department accreditation, and Public Health 3.0: Leveraging opportunities for collaboration. *American Journal of Public Health, 108*, 1334-1340. doi:10.2105/AJPH.2018.304533

Centers of Medicare and Medicaid Services. (2020a). Shared savings program. Retrieved from https://www.cms.gov/Medicare/Medicare-Fee-for-ServicePayment/sharedsavingsprogram/index?redirect=/sharedsavingsprogram/

Centers of Medicare and Medicaid Services. (2020b). ACO Investment Model. Retrieved from https://innovation.cms.gov/initiatives/ACO-Investment-Model/

Centers of Medicare and Medicaid Services. (2020c). Advance Payment ACO Model. Retrieved from https://innovation.cms.gov/initiatives/Advance-Payment-ACO-Model/

Centers of Medicare and Medicaid Services. (2020d). Comprehensive ESRD Care Model. Retrieved from https://innovation.cms.gov/initiatives/comprehensive-ESRD-care/

Centers of Medicare and Medicaid Services. (2020e). Pioneer ACO Model. Retrieved from https://innovation.cms.gov/initiatives/Pioneer-ACO-Model/

Centers of Medicare and Medicaid Services. (2020f). Vermont All-Payer ACO Model. Retrieved from https://innovation.cms.gov/initiatives/vermont-all-payer-aco-model/

Centers of Medicare and Medicaid Services. (2020g). Next Generation ACO Model. Retrieved from https://innovation.cms.gov/initiatives/Next-Generation-ACO-Model/

Centers of Medicare and Medicaid Services. (2018). Medicare Shared Savings Program: Accountable care organization (ACO) 2018 quality measures. Retrieved from https://www.cms.gov/Medicare/Medicare-Fee-for-Service-Payment/sharedsavingsprogram/Downloads/2018-reporting-year-narrative-specifications.pdf

D'Aunno, T., Broffman, L., Sparer, M., & Kumar, S. R. (2018). Factors that distinguish high-performing accountable care organizations in the Medicare Shared Savings Program. *Health Services Research, 53*(1), 120-137. doi:10.1111/1475-6773.12642.

DeCamp, M., Farber, N. J., Torke, A. M., George, M., Berger, Z., Keirns, C., & Kaldjian, L. C. (2014). Ethical challenges for accountable care organizations: A structured review. *Journal of General Internal Medicine, 29,* 1392-1399. doi:10.1007/s11606-014-2833-x

Gensinger, R. A. (2014). *Analytics in health care: An introduction.* Chicago, IL: Health care Information and Management Systems Society.

Gray, C., & Sheiko, S. (2016). Choosing the right performance management system for your ACO. *Physician Leadership Journal, 3*(5), 58-60.

Japinga, M., Alexander, M., & McClellan, M. B. (2019, Winter Supplement). Value-based payment reform for serious illness: Highlighting progress and evidence-based steps that could accelerate the transformation of serious illness care. *Generations–Journal of the American Society of Aging,* 35-41.

Madsen, L. B. (2014). *Data-driven health care: How analytics and BI are transforming the industry.* Hoboken, NJ: Wiley & Sons.

McAlearney, A. S., Walker, D. M., & Hefner. J. L. (2018). Moving organizational culture from volume to value: A qualitative analysis of private sector accountable care organization development. *Health Services Research, 53,* 4767-4788.

National Association of ACOs. (2018). 2016 updates: MSSP Savings Estimates: Program financial performance 2013-2016. Retrieved from https://naacos.memberclicks.net/assets/docs/pdf/AsTreatedDID-SavingsEstimateReport2016.pdf

Ingram, R., Scutchfield, F. D., & Costich, J. F. (2015). Public health department and Accountable Care Organizations: Finding common ground in population health. *American Journal of Public Health, 105,* 840-846. doi:10.2105/AJPH.2014.302483.

Institute for Health Improvement. (2020). The IHI Triple Aim. Retrieved from http://www.ihi.org/Engage/Initiatives/TripleAim/Pages/default.aspx

Office of Inspector General of the U.S. Department of Health and Human Services. (2019). ACOs' strategies for transitioning to value-based care: Lessons from the Medicare Shared Savings Program. Retrieved from https://oig.hhs.gov/oei/reports/oei-02-15-00451.pdf

Office of the National Coordinator for Health Information Technology. (2019). Office-based physician electronic health record adoption. Retrieved from https://dashboard.healthit.gov/quickstats/pages/physician-ehr-adoption-trends.php

Olden, P. C. (2019). *Management of healthcare organizations: An introduction* (3rd ed.). Chicago, IL: Health Administration Press.

Pennic, F. (2018). The state of value-based care in 2018: 10 key trends to know. Retrieved from https://hitconsultant.net/2018/06/18/value-based-care-trends/#.Xl3WfqhKjIV

Williams, S. B. (2016). Strategic plan for maximizing shared savings in accountable care organizations. *Journal of Health care Management, 61*(4), 261-270.

About the Author...

Dr. Alla O. Adams resides in the historic town of Pearland, Texas. She is Assistant Professor of Health care Administration and MHA Program Director at Park University. Dr. Adams has strategic and operational management experience gained from working at academic medical centers such as the University of Texas M. D. Anderson Cancer Center, and the University Medical Center Hamburg-Eppendorf. Her experience has been focused on regulatory compliance, financial analysis, operational flow, grant budgeting, cancer care clinical guidelines, strategic global growth, and international medical services contracts. She also served as a principal consultant at M. D. Anderson Physicians Network, where she engineered a model for separating fixed and variable administrative costs, and developed recommendations on data usage for assessing operational costs, budgeting, and negotiating managed care contracts.

She serves on Ph.D. dissertation committees in the disciplines of Health and Human Services and Health care Administration. Dr. Adams earned her Doctor of Philosophy in Health care Administration from Capella University, Master of Science in Health care Administration from Houston Baptist University, and Master of Science in Public Health and Epidemiology from Kiev Institute of Medicine.

To reach Dr. Alla Adams for additional information or guest speaking, **e-mail: aadams@park.edu**

CHAPTER 7

Enhancing Group Dynamics and Project Success Through Situational Leadership Lens

Dr. Gail Ade & Dr. Alan L. Bundschuh Jr.

The growth forecast for the project management discipline is immense; a colossal estimate of more than 80 million project management professionals by 2027 (The Project Management Institute [PMI], 2017). Unrelenting pressure for speed, quality, accuracy, cost reduction, and improved performance coupled with the ongoing socio-economic developments are the underlining catalysts increasing the demands for project management practitioners in the global marketplace (Cesarotti, Gubinelli, & Introna, 2019; Dolata, 2019). Yet, as the project-oriented industries grow, new challenges and burdens emerge (Ballesteros-Sánchez, Ortiz-Marcos, & Rodríguez-Rivero, 2019). In addition, the rate of project failure is also alarming. According to Alami (2016), the majority of projects fail in one capacity or another, projects more than $1 million have a 50% higher rate of failure, and most companies have experienced at least one project failure. Through refractive thinking, the information in this chapter highlights foundational insights into the project management landscape through a situational leadership lens, as well as the leadership styles relevant to the different project lifecycles. Subsequent information includes a synthesis of relationship-enhancing and task-oriented skills, such as agility, collective efficacy, technical expertise, psychological safety, emotional intelligence, situational awareness, and conflict management.

The contemporary global business environment continues to generate fierce competition, disruptive technologies, artificial intelligence (AI), relational complexities, strategic dynamism, challenging market conditions, and situational ambiguities (Conforto, Amaral, da Silva, Di Felippo & Kamikawachi, 2016; Cesarotti et al., 2019; Dolata, 2019). Organizational viability, profitability, and sustainability depend on multidimensional foresight, strategic positioning, creative group efficacy, adaptable leadership excellence, and the meta-abilities to maximize resources, including the human capital (Dolata, 2019; Jeffs & Papillon, 2019; Krusi & Whitty, 2019). The 21st-century business reality necessitates aligning project goals with organizational business strategy, which is essential to sustain a competitive edge and profitable outcomes. Furthermore, focusing on the core leadership models that motivate and inclusively engage teams are pivotal to project success and optimal group dynamics (Ballesteros-Sánchez et al., 2019; Krusi & Whitty, 2019). With such high rate intricacies shaping the project management industry, practitioners and researchers can no longer ignore the influence of project manager's leadership style and relational competencies to project success (Malakyan, 2018; Shao, 2018). Consequently, project management continues to be of high research interest across the top industries.

The PMI defined projects as temporary ventures undertaken to produce specific goods or services using project management methodologies (time, budget, and scope) and industry best practices. Project management involves multiple stakeholders using various resources such as time, assets, money, and human capital for project actualization. Throughout the lifecycle of each project, the project managers are responsible for project objectives, optimizing team dynamics, and cultivating successful project outcomes. Project managers distribute project-specific responsibilities and use project portfolio management to coordinate various tasks amid several risks. Project risks can fluctuate between simple complications, difficulties, or even result in problematic chaos, depending on the circumstances. Such diverse responsibilities imply that project managers must be versatile as situationally needed to foster positive team dynamics and successful project results.

Successful project completion relies on the productivity of a temporarily assembled group of people working within a limited time, budget, and scope (Furukawa, 2016). Delivering the complete project scope at or below cost, on or ahead of schedule, and with acceptable quality is the final measure of success for project managers and their teams. The iron triangle or triple constraint of scope, schedule, and cost were the criteria for measuring project realization in the past. Quality is the latest constraint accepted as a measure of project success. The PMI (2017) posited that a successful project must meet the following criteria:

a. Timely delivery.

b. Within the budget.

c. Useful and Valuable.

d. Expected quality.

e. Satisfactory to funding stakeholders or sponsors.

There are several barriers to successful project completion. A common obstacle that project managers encounter is the lack of scope clarity, i.e., not understanding what the sponsors and customers want from the project (Ajmal, Khan, & Al-Yafei, 2019; Antony & Gupta, 2019). Resources in the form of human capital, equipment, and supplies are often limited or inadequate

(Antony & Gupta, 2019; Kim, Chang, & Castro-Lacouture, 2020). The usability of the final product or service is another barrier to delivering a successful project. Sometimes, projects may be unsuccessful even if the project team delivered the goods or services on time, at cost, within the required scope and quality. In some cases, even when a project meets all deliverables, the product produced may not suffice if it is not the first available to the public. For example, a software project that meets the constraint parameters just days or weeks after another company introduced a similar product to the open market.

Strategic reasons for why project teams are unsuccessful include improper planning, lack of experience, mismatched human capital, inept leadership abilities, and poor management skills (Ballesteros-Sánchez et al., 2019). Lack of communication, interpersonal shortcomings, little to no employee engagement, low productivity, and weak relationships are top tactical reasons why teams collapse (Ballesteros-Sánchez et al., 2019). Incorrect leadership styles also inhibit project teams from working at optimal performance levels. Using the wrong leadership style or implementing an arbitrary command and control style of leadership style in an unmotivated or unskilled team environment can be a massive detriment to team delivery and performance. Therefore, seeking additional knowledge of the applicable leadership styles for enhancing group dynamics and project success is necessary.

Project Management Stages and Relevant Leadership Styles

Project managers hold significant power as the architect of project success, whose actions or inaction can have intended and unintentional outcomes (Ahmed & Anantatmula, 2017). Whether planning for a new consumer product, software package, office building, or work process, putting the right leadership in place at the right time is vital for success. If timed and implemented well, diverse leadership styles can increase the likelihood of project success and enrich team performance, efficacy, and workflow (Teoh, Coyne, Devonish, Leather, & Zarola, 2016; Wingerden, Bakker, & Derks, 2016). However, a wide variety of leadership styles exist, ranging from laissez-faire, transactional, transformational, visionary, authentic leadership, and many others. As a result, it is important to explore various leadership styles relevant to the different project management stages (development, implementation, and completion).

Project Management Stages

During the *feasibility and conceptual stage* of the project, when the team and sponsors work together to identify all pertinent scope, a *visionary leadership style* may be the best approach. The preliminary stage of project management involves introducing the proactive project vision and conceiving the larger picture necessary to establish buy-ins, confidence, and alliance among project teams. With few requirements or specific deliverables, engaging project teams around a shared vision creates room for creativity and innovation to thrive (Choi, Kim, Ebrahim Ullah, & Kang, 2016). Transformational or relationship-oriented leadership style might be necessary to cultivate team-building and prospective confidence from the project outlook (Ngqibi & Sines, 2019). The passionate manner employed by inspirational leaders to present the project vision can generate enthusiasm and redirect focus on productive interactions (Bundschuh, 2018; Perev, 2018). Even seasoned project practitioners can rally behind a visionary leader as they begin planning the project work and timing. Transformational or charismatic leadership provides intrinsic motivation, which leads to increased team performance and positive employee outcomes (Kuvaas, Buch, Weibel, Dysvik, & Nerstad, 2017).

As the project moves toward a *definition and design phase*, a shift in leadership style is likely necessary. Defining project plans and developing precise steps happen during the planning phase. Team members have distinct roles to play and specific parts to deliver; therefore, laying out individual roles and specific responsibilities are principal to team and project success. Beyond preparations and strategy, the planning phase also details the information about risk, rewards, alignment, and project sponsorship. Project leaders can implement *transactional or task-oriented leadership style* to predetermine work overview. Metering out rewards or perceived punishments according to the leaders' expectations and task completion is the hallmark of transactional leadership. Team leaders measure completed or in-process contributions of each team member to gauge performance level, offer directives to those struggling with assigned tasks or reprimand as needed to reset the course of direction (Saravo, Netzel, & Kiesewetter, 2017). Transactional leaders also promote compliance by leveraging a systematic check and balance system for enhanced motivation and productivity. Just as sponsors engage teams to map out directions and strategies for project goals, the check and balance style of transactional leadership reinforces motivation when teams are experiencing difficulty in meeting project deliverables.

    The *construction phase* of the project puts all the previous stages into action. The execution stage of project management is where the proverbial rubber meets the road. One or more leadership styles may be beneficial to keep the vision alive and sustain relevance. Strategic leadership might be necessary to ensure project implementation aligns with organizational business strategy. Measuring tasks and deliverables helps to determine whether the project is on or off schedule. Shared leadership will encourage project teams to contribute freely and participate in the decision-making process. A hands-off approach known as laissez-faire may foster creativity on the part of each team member and lead to a better project outcome. The laissez-faire leadership style may provide the project teams with the autonomy to take any suitable approach to complete the assigned project task. The hands-off approach may also be appropriate early in the project when teams are forming project vision or later during the design and construction phases. The refractive thinking insight is that no single leadership style is a one-size-fits-all approach when managing projects and diverse project teams. Versatile project leaders must be mindful of what leadership styles to apply, what combination, and when to shift between the specific paradigms.

No definitive leadership style is best when leading projects. Project success and positive team dynamics necessitate open-mindedness and multidimensional capacity to meet a project, team, and situational needs (Henkel, Marion, & Bourdeau, 2019). As evident in the plethora of research studies, the best leaders use a mixture of several styles and skills in varying degrees at different phases of a project lifecycle (Henkel et al., 2019). Just as all projects are ad-hoc endeavors aimed at delivering specific goals and requirements, project leadership is also an ad-hoc endeavor mastery of which leadership styles to mix, when, and how to help teams navigate the project landscape.

Project Management Through a Situational Leadership Lens

According to the situational leadership theory, a leadership model debuted in 1969 by Ken Blanchard and Paul Hersey; there is no right or wrong leadership style (Wright, 2017). Instead, leaders need to be cognizant and receptive to diverse leadership styles as situationally required, considering the type of task, groups, and situational needs (Malakyan, 2018). The premise of situational leadership is that circumstances change often, and different needs emerge as a result. As a result, leaders must embrace a flexible mindset when overseeing project teams and acclimatizing to the changing conditions and emerging needs (Yeo, 2018).

According to Yeo (2018), situational leadership theory highlights the following underlying assumptions:

a. Leaders have multiple styles of influence.

b. Leaders can adapt behavior to meet the demands of each distinct situation.

c. Leaders also have dual capabilities to direct and support.

d. Leadership embodies tasks (job / performance) and relationship (valued interaction) responsibilities.

Through the project management lens, situational leadership underpins the resourcefulness in balancing directive and supportive responsibilities when combating the various tasks associated with completing projects and influencing the assigned project teams (Malakyan, 2018; Wright, 2017). The basic principles of the situational leadership framework require competent program managers to espouse multiple leadership styles, managerial expertise, and interpersonal skills to impact a clear vision, enthusiasm, and transformational influence across the team (Henkel et al., 2019; Malakyan, 2018; Yeo, 2018). The responsibilities of project managers, under the situational leadership model, are feasible through a fusion of the task-oriented and relationship-oriented leadership competencies discussed below.

Task-oriented Competencies for Project Managers

Task-oriented skills relate to organizational design, scheme, direction, and established practices for attaining missions and objectives (Battilana, Gilmartin, Sengul, Pache, & Alexander, 2010).

Task duties include determining / coordinating team members' roles, clarifying job requirements, lessening risk, and ensuring project completion within the pre-established timeline (Tognazzo, Gubitta, & Gerli, 2017). Effectiveness at task-oriented behaviors hinges on the strategic foresight of project managers to align project goals to the organizational purpose (Battilana et al., 2010). Task-oriented behaviors also include emphasizing efficiency and reliability, maximizing resources, removing roadblocks, and establishing priorities, despite the market conditions (Tognazzo et al., 2017).

Examples of Task-oriented Skills:

Technical expertise is the most significant hallmark of project management. Somewhat why past researchers mostly featured the technical reasons why projects fail (Ballesteros-Sánchez et al., 2019). Notwithstanding additional qualifications, project teams and managers need *hard technical* skills to successfully execute the structure, lifecycle, portfolio, and accessibility of any project. From the beginning of the project, managing an agile team is another requisite for achieving group dynamics and project success. *Agility* (the ability to move swiftly) in managers, teams, and proficiencies will lead to better project and product performance (Cesarotti et al., 2019; Conforto et al., 2016). According to Fan, Lima, and Rocha (2018), agile groups are more reliable and versatile to endure unexpected changes and challenges that result from limited resources and cost constraints. Another distinct team success fundamental is ensuring *collective efficacy*, which is the perceived skill level and capabilities of a team to perform desired tasks at a higher level (Murray, Coffee, Arthur, & Eklund, 2019). According to Fan et al. (2018), group efficacy predicts behavior trends and degree of cooperation, in addition to breeding self-managed teams in work settings.

Relationship-oriented Competencies for Project Managers

Person-oriented skills include leadership behaviors that promote collaborative interaction among team members, establish a supportive social climate, and strengthen management conducts that ensure equitable treatment of all (Battilana et al., 2010; Tognazzo et al., 2017). Relationship-oriented practices also include support and empowerment through coaching and mentoring, as well as recognizing contributions and celebrating achievements (Tognazzo et al., 2017). Effectual person-oriented behaviors rely on the ability to show consideration for personal and other people's emotions to sustain positive interactions (Battilana et al., 2010). Below are strategic proficiencies and interpersonal skills that encompass person-oriented behaviors.

Examples of Relationship-oriented Skills

Every stage of a project lifecycle is contingent on the interactions between diverse stakeholders, open and active communication pathways are pivotal to the outcome (Jeffs & Papillon, 2019). *Communication* is fundamental to project management success, stakeholder engagement, and team interaction (Osborne & Hammoud, 2017). The aptitude to communicate effectively is integrally universal for all leaders. Without real communication, project managers will not properly articulate project vision, implement the right strategies, or finish projects on time and within budget (Jeffs & Papillon, 2019).

Moving the teams through each stage of the project life cycle requires the ability to resolve misunderstandings and *mitigate conflict*, which is bound to occur as teams consist of individuals with distinct worldviews (Liu, Chen, Jiang, & Klein, 2010). Bringing together disparate views and dealing with conflict head-on is vital for team management (Liu et al., 2010). Effectively managing conflict is fundamental to reduce tension among teammates, but also integral to cultivating a *psychologically safe team environment*, where members can be authentic without any fear of retribution for expressing thoughts or concerns (Ade, Majaro, & Poshi, 2019). Such respectful and supportive team environments help cultivate trust-building, transparency, collaboration, and well-functioning relationships.

Drawing upon behavioral principles of decision making and situational influence, *inclusive leadership* provides a sense of belonging, stimulates motivation, and translates group efficiency into project success (Wu, Kwan, Yim, Chiu, & He, 2015). Pooled leadership, according to expertise and tactical skills, will foster coordinated preparation, collaborative decision-making, and knowledge sharing useful beyond the project lifecycle (Scott-Young, Georgy, & Grisinger, 2019). Incorporating team input into multiple-stakeholder initiatives fosters inclusive engagement and collaborative work climates (Ade et al., 2019; Wu et al., 2015). As a result, inspiring all team members to perform at the best of their capabilities is an inherent stipulation for boosting autonomy, innovation, and performance (Senaratne & Samaraweera, 2015).

All project management strategies should be adapted accordingly to the distinctive characteristics of the project goal, team, and environment. However, the global business environment is never constant; ongoing change is the current norm. Consequently, multilevel decision-making and tactical foresight necessitate *situational awareness*, which is an insightful awakening with the explicit-tacit perception of current dynamics (Parse, 2020; Tower, Watson, Bourke, Tyers, & Tin, 2019). Situational refers to immediate or contextual surroundings, while awareness implies discerning acumen (Parse, 2020). Both of which are the indicative precursor of strategic and operational excellence (Tower et al., 2019).

Awareness, like many behavioral leadership skills, relies on some degree of emotional acuity. *Emotional intelligence* is the mindful ability to recognize and self-regulate personal emotions, become receptive to the feelings of others, and empathically harness social relationships for situational purposes (Nadiia, Boris, Sergey, & Alina, 2019; Osborne & Hammoud, 2017). Tolerating people's differences during interactions and power dynamics are also components of emotional intelligence that contributes to group productivity. Emotionally intelligent leaders leverage self-consciousness, compassion and attentiveness to enhance optimism and boost productive behaviors in teams (Nadiia et al., 2019; Osborne & Hammoud, 2017).

Recommendations for Project Management Practitioners

As a direct implication of the ongoing socio-economic developments in the 21st-century business environment, ongoing competency development is fundamental for project management practitioners. While conventional project management training programs emphasize routine technical skills, managing a series of steps to complete a project is no longer sufficient to meet the modern-day business demands. Through continuous leadership training, certification programs, and work experiences, program managers can hone their expertise beyond technical or theoretical capacity. As such, progressive project managers will balance tactical knowledge with adaptable leadership skills and team management expertise in appropriate circumstances. According to the 2017 Project Management Body of Knowledge (PMBOK®), these humanistic considerations as the present keystone of successful project management and the preemptive focus of ongoing competency improvement (Shao, 2018). To effectively boost team dynamics and reinforce project success, skilled leaders must exercise these refractive thinking strategies throughout the project lifespan:

a. Building commitment and confidence to achieve project objectives.

b. Keeping project vision, purpose, and approach relevant and meaningful.

c. Managing relationships and mitigating performance-hindering problems.

d. Providing opportunities for team members to enhance their skills continuously.

Conclusion

In a globally connected world driven by fierce market competition, disruptive technologies, fluctuating market conditions, AI, paradoxes, and shifting social dynamics, no single leadership style is universally superior or deemed sufficient alone. Several research studies indicated that the best leaders would mix several leadership styles, hardcore technical skills, and strategic management expertise in varying degrees to meet specific project, team, and situational needs. The refractive thinking message is clear; versatile project leaders who are highly skilled in both relationship and task-oriented management will favorably leverage situational leadership capabilities for organizational excellence and sustainable success. All the behavior, cognitive, and social skills discussed in this chapter are acquirable over time through coaching, training, mentoring, and proficiency development. The leadership implication is that agile leaders who are profoundly capable of positively influencing team dynamics and executing projects will be a competitive advantage and top sought-after expertise across many industries.

THOUGHTS FROM THE ACADEMIC ENTREPRENEUR

The Problem to be Solved:

- Improving group dynamics and project success through situational leadership lens.

The goals:

- Understanding how to increase project success through various tools, leadership styles, and management of group dynamics.

The Questions to Ask:

- How can organizations enhance group dynamics and increase project success through situational leadership paradigm?
- Can multiple leadership styles improve project lifecycle stages?

Today's Business Application:

- No single leadership style is universally superior or adequate alone when managing projects and project teams.
- Flexible project leaders who are proficient in both relationship and task-oriented management are better equipped to lead project success and positive group dynamics.
- Aligning project goals with organizational business strategy will foster productivity, competitive advantage and sustainable success.

REFERENCES

Ade, G., Majaro, T., & Poshi, M. (2019). The refractive thinker® Vol XVI: Generations: Strategies for managing generations in the workforce. In C. Lentz (Ed.), *Chapter 8: Multigenerational leadership & engagement: A balancing act for 21st century leaders* (pp. 151–163). Grayslake, IL: The Refractive Thinker® Press.

Ahmed, R., & Anantatmula, V. (2017). Empirical study of project managers leadership competence and project performance. *Engineering Management Journal, 29*(3), 189-205. doi:10.1080/10429247.2017.1343005

Alami, A. (2016). Why do information technology projects fail? *Procedia Computer Science, 100,* 62–71. doi:10.1016/j.procs.2016.09.124

Ballesteros-Sánchez, L., Ortiz-Marcos, I., & Rodríguez-Rivero, R. (2019). The impact of executive coaching on project managers' personal competencies. *Project Management Journal, 50*(3), 306. doi:10.1177/8756972819832191

Battilana, J., Gilmartin, M., Sengul, M., Pache, A., & Alexander, J. A. (2010). Leadership competencies for implementing planned organizational change. *The Leadership Quarterly, 21,* 422–438. doi:10.1016/j.leaqua.2010.03.007

Bundschuh, A. (2018). *Relationships between project cost, project team member role, project schedule, and burnout* (Doctoral dissertation). Retrieved from ProQuest Dissertations& Thesis database. (UMI No. 10822093)

Choi, S. B., Kim, K., Ebrahim Ullah, S. M., & Kang, S. (2016) How transformational leadership facilitates innovative behavior of Korean workers: Examining mediating and moderating processes, *Personnel Review, 45,* 459–479. doi:10.1108/PR-03-2014-0058

Cesarotti, V., Gubinelli, S., & Introna, V. (2019). The evolution of project management (PM): How agile, lean and Six Sigma are changing PM. *Journal of Modern Project Management, 7*(3), 1–29. doi:10.19255/JMPM02107

Conforto, E., Amaral, D., da Silva, S., Di Felippo, A., & Kamikawachi, D. (2016). The agility construct on project management theory. *International Journal of Project Management, 34,* 660–674. doi:10.1016/j.ijproman.2016.01.007

Dolata, M. (2019). The sources of competitive advantage from the perspective of project management - results of empirical studies. *Management 23*(1), 75–89. doi:10.2478/manment-2019-0005

Fan, P., Lima, S., & Rocha, Á. (2018). Research on the collective efficacy of social networks with multi factor analysis. *Journal of Intelligent & Fuzzy Systems, 35,* 2827–2836. doi:10.3233/JIFS-169636

Furukawa, C. (2016). Dynamics of a critical problem-solving project team and creativity in a multiple-project environment. *Team Performance Management, 22*(1/2), 92–110. doi:10.1108/TPM-04-2015-0021

Henkel, T. G., Marion, J. W., & Bourdeau, D. T. (2019). Project manager leadership behavior: Task-oriented versus relationship-oriented. *Journal of Leadership Education, 18*(2). doi.10.12806/V18/I2/ R8

Jeffs, J., & Papillon, B. (2019). Globalization, the new economy and project management: A graph theory perspective. *Journal of Modern Project Management, 7*(3), 118–146. doi:10.19255/JMPM02007

Krusi, M., & Whitty, S. J. (2019). The practitioner's tapestry: Revealing the epistemological diversity to project management knowledge. *Journal of Modern Project Management, 7*(3), 196–226. doi:10.19255/JMPM02010

Kuvaas, B., Buch, R., Weibel, A., Dysvik, A., & Nerstad, C. G. L. (2017). Do intrinsic and extrinsic motivation relate differently to employee outcomes? *Journal of Economic Psychology, 61,* 244–258. doi:10.1016/j.joep.2017.05.004

Liu, J., Chen, H., Jiang, J., & Klein, G. (2010). Task completion competency and project management performance: The influence of control and user contribution. *International Journal of Project Management, 28*(3), 220–227. doi:10.1016/j.ijproman.2009.05.006

Malakyan, P. (2018). Envisioning future of leadership and organizations: Putting the new wine within a fresh wineskin. *Journal of Leadership Studies, 12*(4), 71–73. doi:10.1002/jls.21614

Murray, R., Coffee, P., Arthur, C., & Eklund, R. (2019). Social identity moderates the effects of team-referent attributions on collective efficacy but not emotions. *Sport, Exercise, and Performance Psychology.* doi.10.1037/spy0000178.supp doi:10.1177/0146167219893995.

Nadiia, R., Boris, K., Sergey, B., & Alina, Z. (2019). Role of empathy, emotional intelligence, transformational leadership of the project success. *2019 IEEE 14th International Conference on Computer Sciences and Information Technologies (CSIT),* Lviv, Ukraine, 2019, (pp. 116-121). doi:10.1109/ STC-CSIT.2019.8929871

Ngqibi, N. N., & Sines, C. C. (2019). Relationship between idealized leadership behavior and change initiative success. *Journal of International Business and Management, 3*(1), 1–8. doi:10.37227/jibm.2020.32

Osborne, S., & Hammoud, M.S. (2017). Effective employee engagement in the workplace. International *Journal of Applied Management & Technology, 16*(1), 50–67. doi:10.5590/IJAMT.2017.16.1.04

Parse, R. (2020.). Situational awareness: A leadership phenomenon. *Nursing Science Quarterly, 31,* 317–318. doi.10.1177/0894318418792888

Perev, B. (2018). Strategies *Hospitality leaders use to reduce employee turnover* (Doctoral dissertation). Retrieved from ProQuest Dissertations & Thesis database. (UMI No. 10932121)

PMBOK Guide. (2017). *A guide to the project management body of knowledge* (6th ed.). Newtown Square, PA: Project Management Institute.

Project Management Institute (PMI). (2017). Project management job growth and talent gap 2017–2027. Retrieved from http://www.pmi.org

Project Management Institute. (2004). *A guide to the project management body of knowledge (PMBOK guide)*. Newtown Square, PA: Project Management Institute.

Saravo, B., Netzel, J., & Kiesewetter, J. (2017). The need for strong clinical leaders: Transformational and transactional leadership as a framework for resident leadership training. *PLoS ONE 12*(8), 24. doi:10.1371/journal.pone.0183019

Scott-Young, C. M., Georgy, M., & Grisinger, A. (2019). Shared leadership in project teams: An integrative multilevel conceptual model and research agenda. *International Journal of Project Management, 37*, 565–581. doi:10.1016/j.ijproman.2019.02.002

Senaratne, S., & Samaraweera, A. (2015). Construction project leadership across the team development process. *Built Environment Project & Asset Management, 5*(1), 69. doi:10.1108/BEPAM-10-2012-0049

Shao, J. (2018). The moderating effect of program context on the relationship between program managers' leadership competences and program success. *International Journal of Project Management, 36*(1), 108–120. doi:10.1016/j.ijproman.2017.05.004

Teoh, K. R. H., Coyne, I., Devonish, D., Leather, P., & Zarola, A. (2016). The interaction between supportive and unsupportive manager behaviors on employee work attitudes. *Personnel Review, 45*, 1386–1402. doi:10.1108/PR-05-2015-0136

Tognazzo, A., Gubitta, P., & Gerli, F. (2017). Fostering performance through leaders' behavioral competencies. *International Journal of Organizational Analysis, 25*(2), 295. doi:10.1108/IJOA-07-2016-1044

Tower, M., Watson, B., Bourke, A., Tyers, E., & Tin, A. (2019). Situation awareness and the decision-making processes of final-year nursing students. *Journal of Clinical Nursing, 28*, 3923–3934. doi:10.1111/jocn.14988

Wingerden, J. van, Bakker, A. B., & Derks, D. (2016). A test of a job demands-resources intervention. *Journal of Managerial Psychology, 31*, 686–701. doi:10.1108/JMP10203-2014-0086

Wright, E. S. (2017). Dialogic development in the situational leadership style. *Performance Improvement, 56*(9), 27–31. doi:10.1002/pfi.21733

Wu, L., Kwan, H., Yim, F., Chiu, R., & He, X. (2015). CEO ethical leadership and corporate social responsibility: A moderated mediation model. *Journal of Business Ethics, 130*, 819-831. doi:10.1007/s10551-014-2108-9

Yeo, R. K. (2018). Get ready to shift: Situational positioning of leadership identity and influence. *Organizational Dynamics*. doi:10.1016/j.orgdyn.2018.11.001

About the Authors...

Dr. Gail Ade is an ICF credentialed & board-certified executive leadership, business & career coach. Through intentional engagement, She facilitates breakthrough coaching to empower executive leaders (current and emerging), small business owners, professionals, and entrepreneurs to achieve sustainable success. As a social change advocate, Dr. Ade also partners with organizations to advance diversity beyond representation.

Dr. Ade earned her Doctor of Business Administration (DBA) in Organizational Leadership, and Master of Business Administration (MBA) in Human Resource Management. She also holds a Ph.D. Bridge to Management in Leadership & Organizational Strategy, as well as a Graduate Certificate in Industrial & Organizational Psychology.

Dr. Ade is an active member of the Society for Human Resource Management (SHRM), International Coach Federation (ICF), National Society of Leadership & Success, and Society for Diversity.

To reach Dr. Gail Ade, please **e-mail**: **dradegail@gmail.com**

Dr. Alan L. Bundschuh Jr. resides in Delaware. He is an Adjunct Instructor at Delaware Technical and Community College and an Associate Clinical Professor at Southern Illinois University Carbondale. He works as a Capital Systems, Project and Construction Manager at Procter & Gamble and is an active member of the Delaware Valley Chapter of the Project Management Institute.

Published works include his doctoral study: *Relationships Between Project Cost, Project Team Member Role, Project Schedule, and Burnout*. Dr. Alan earned his Doctor of Business Administration (DBA) with a concentration in Project Management and his Master of Business Administration (MBA) with a concentration in Leadership. Dr. Alan has volunteered and coached with 4-H, Junior Achievement, and Odyssey of the Mind along with numerous youth sports teams.

To reach Dr. Alan L. Bundschuh Jr., please **e-mail**: **drabundschuh@gmail.com** or visit **Linked-In: www.linkedin.com/in/alan-bundschuh-dba-5233827**

CHAPTER 8

Help Wanted: Strategies for Hiring Your Perfect Project Manager

Dr. Natalie Casale

According to the U.S. Bureau of Labor Statistics (BLS) (2020) Job Openings and Labor Turnover Survey (JOLTS), the number of job openings decreased by 6.4 million and the job openings rate decreased by 4% in December 2019. The number of hires (5.9 million; 3.9%) and separations (5.7 million; 3.8%) has remained consistent throughout 2019 (U.S. Bureau of Labor Statistics [U.S. BLS], 2020). Because the number of hires is more than the number of separations, employment has increased (U.S. BLS, 2020). According to the U.S. BLS JOLTS, the net employment gain was 2.2 million in 2019. According to the Project Management Institute (PMI) (2017b), there is an increase in project-oriented organizations because the popularity of a global economy; therefore, the need for qualified project managers will become more critical. The growing concern among the company leaders of these project-oriented companies is the lack of qualified and skilled project managers to fill open project management positions (Project Management Institute [PMI], 2017b). With the growing number of jobs in the United States (U.S. BLS, 2020) and the need for skilled project manager positions (PMI, 2017b), the goal of this chapter is to use the Refractive Thinker® approach to investigate the effective strategies a hiring manager and business leader uses to find the perfect project manager.

The focus of this chapter is to identify strategies a hiring manager and a business leader can use to hire a project manager that fits the needs of the business and project(s). The specific business problem is that some leaders do not know what strategies work best to hire the perfect project manager. Understanding the business needs and project charter will help the hiring manager determine the best project manager for the position.

Defining What is a Project Manager

Several organizational leaders provide standards, services, information, networks, and processes for a person to develop into a good project manager. The most known is the PMI, established in 1969 (PMI, 2020a). The executive leadership team of the PMI provides resources, tools, and networks for professionals in project management positions (PMI, 2020a). A project management professional would be most interested in the Project Management Profession (PMP) certification. PMI employees designed the PMP certification exam to test a project manager about five process groups (initiating, planning, executing, monitoring / controlling, and closing), 10 knowledge areas (integration, scope, schedule, cost, quality, resource, communications, risk, procurement, and stakeholders), and 47 processes project manager should know to do to their job well (PMI, 2020b). An alternative to the PMP is the certified associate in project management certification (CAPM) (PMI, 2020b). An entry-level project manager not established in the project management field would find the CAPM beneficial because he or she can demonstrate the understanding of the project management standards and meet the number of years experienced qualifications (PMI, 2020b).

Before PMI, was a global organization that provided similar resources. The International Project Management Association

(IPMA) was established in 1965 to provide global standards for project management professionals (IPMA, 2020a). The IPMA (2020a) is a federation comprised of 70 member associations for each participating nation. Project managers working in global organizations that need a network, information, and standards between other global organizations, government agencies, and universities would find the IPMA most useful for their professional needs and success for running projects (IPMA, 2020a). The IPMA certification exam has three competencies: perspective, people, and practice (IPMA, 2020b). Within these three competencies are 29 competence elements further divided into knowledge, skills, and abilities an individual will need to know to complete a project successfully (IPMA, 2020b).

Project in Controlled Environments, version 2 (PRINCE2), is a popular method used by project managers in the United Kingdom, Australia, and Western European countries (Axelos, n.d.). The PRINCE2 Practitioner certification exam includes questions that break down the project manager role into six performance goals (timescales, costs, quality, scope, benefits, and risk), seven principles or mindsets that a project manager cannot alter, seven themes (business case, organization, quality, plans, risks, change, and progress) (Axelos, n.d.). Pre-qualifications to take the exam include certification in CAPM or IPMA (Axelos, n.d.).

The PMI, IPMA, and Axelos provide practitioner certification exams that hiring managers/business leaders use to list in a project manager job opportunity as a requirement or preferred qualification for the position. What the PMI (2020b) PMP certification exam, IPMA (2020b) certification exam, and PRINCE2 have in common is there needs to be a set of standards any project manager can follow to run a project successfully. Both the PMI and IPMA organizational leaders stress the importance of ethics, professional conduct, and stakeholder satisfaction.

The Role of a Project Manager

Before hiring a project manager, the human resources manager (HRM) and business leader should know the role the project manager is needed for a position, ensuring project success. A project manager is a change agent (PMI, 2017a). According to PMI (2017a), the project manager should be assigned to a project during the initiating process group, knowledge area integration, and the process to develop the project charter. The sooner a project manager is assigned to the project, the faster the project manager can begin implementing the 47 processes that may be needed to complete the project (PMI, 2017a). Throughout the project, the project manager ensures the project remains in alignment with the business needs by maintaining documented information, such as an issues log, lessons learned, and risk register (PMI, 2017a).

The project manager role is different from the project expeditor and project coordinator but has similarities. The project expeditor manages a project; however, responsible for coordinating communications and does not have the authority to make decisions about the project (PMI, 2017a). The project coordinator's role is similar to the project expeditor except does have some power to make decisions on the project; however, not all choices as a project manager does (PMI, 2017a). Understanding the level of authority will help the hiring manager determine the precise role to identify in the job opening.

Project Success

A hiring manager should understand what a project is before determining the skills required a candidate should have to ensure project success. According to PMI (2017a), a project has a target date, completing as closed or canceled. A project is temporary (PMI, 2017a); therefore, the project manager's position could be, also. The hiring manager needs to know if the job requires the project manager candidate for one project and time length or many projects after that. A project manager may need a few to all processes to complete a project (PMI, 2017a). Understanding the 10 knowledge areas will help the hiring manager determine the required skills for the position. For example, not all projects need a person to select or interact with vendors. A project manager candidate who is most knowledgeable in this area may not be the best fit for the job.

Project leaders complete a project either successfully or unsuccessfully. Understanding what determines project success can help the hiring manager list the desired skills needed by the project manager candidate to meet this goal. Millhollan and Kaarst-Brown (2016) determined project success has three categories: project outcomes, project management processes, and the influence of the project manager. Project success factors of project outcomes can include outcomes during or after the project and a potential conflict of measurements or perceptions (Millhollan & Kaarst-Brown, 2016). A project is successful when the outcome of the business objectives of the project are met (Millhollan & Kaarst-Brown, 2016). The project management processes are the knowledge and understanding of the 47 processes defined in the PMBOK (PMI, 2017a). Maintaining a PMP or CAPM certificate will confirm the project manager candidate understands project management processes.

A project can have many risks, leading to project failure. Project managers use project management methodologies, such as Kanban, Scrum, Lean, Waterfall, and Agile, to ensure project success. Pace (2019) conducted a correlational study, using a survey instrument that included questions for the participant to categorize project outcomes as successful or less than successful. The sample population consisted of 367 project managers in the North America region, 25 years or older with 5 years' experience with multiple methodologies (Pace, 2019). Each participant was PMP certified (Pace, 2019). Pace concluded there is a weak correlation between project management methodologies and project success. Pace suggested other variables, such as the adaption, maturation, or tailing of project management processes, not project management methodologies is more critical to project success. Most company leaders use PMBOK® as a base, altering processes to fit their particular business needs. A project manager that can do the same during the project processes may prove more valuable than understanding the project management methodologies.

In October 1984, the first PMP exam was offered (PMI, 2020b). As of 2019, one million people passed the PMP exam and maintained their project management certification status (PMI, 2020b). The number of certified and uncertified project managers continues to grow (PMI, 2017b); therefore, some hiring managers may be concerned with the age of a potential candidate. Hoxha and McMahan (2019) conducted a correlational study of the project manager's age and project success. Hoxha and McMahan used the project implementation profile (PIP) survey, questioning 108 participants in Albania and Kosovo. Hoxha and McMahan concluded no significant relationship existed between a project manager's work experience and project success; therefore, the project manager's age does not impact project success. Hoxha and McMahan suggested project managers should not be discriminated based on age. Therefore, age should not be a factor when selecting potential candidates for a project management position.

Hiring a Project Manager

Hiring a project manager can be a daunting task. According to the U.S. BLS (2020), the number of job openings continues to increase. The problem many people are applying for the same position. In 2020, although the number of job openings exceeded the number of unemployed, many employed people are looking for better jobs that pay more or better meet their skills and education. With a plethora of people job hunting, what strategies would ensure hiring a perfect project manager?

A hiring manager should know what type of project manager is needed to fulfill the job opening and meet business needs. Zwikael and Meredith (2017) analyzed the key terms that define who is a project manager, project team, project management office, program manager, customer, sponsor, and champion. Zwikael and Meredith concluded these terms were not used consistently in meaning. Inconsistent terminology for common project managers' inputs, tools, and outputs may confuse the project manager who transfers jobs. The problem already exists that people do not apply for positions they meet the required skills (Leonard, 2019). A job opening should contain detail of the type of project manager the hiring manager needs, and the critical roles expected for the project to avoid additional candidates applying for a position that does not match their experiences or skills.

According to PMI (2020b), a project manager should know 47 processes to manage a project successfully; however, the project manager may not need all 47 processes for the project. The hiring manager should create a required skills list that meets the need of the project. Ahsan, Ho, and Khan (2013) reviewed 762 open job positions for a different level of project managers in a variety of industries in Australia and New Zealand. Ahsan et al. captured data that applied to the knowledge, skills, and abilities (KSA) model. Ahsan et al.'s data results portrayed communication the most sought out KSA, at 61.68%; followed by technical skills (43.47%), stakeholder management (41.73%), cost management (37.40%), time management (32.68%), education background (28.61%), planning, (26.12%) leadership (24.41%), team build and management (22.57%), and certification (20.47%). Good communication skills of a project manager were defined as the ability to report, present, develop relationships with management and leadership, and interpersonal skills effectively (Ahsan et al., 2013). Included in the data collection were project managers from a variety of industries; however, technical skills were relevant for project managers in technical positions (Ahsan et al., 2013). According to Leonard (2019), candidates should provide their accomplishments instead of skills. Candidates should be specific has to how they accomplished effective communication managing a successful project. Also, a candidate applying for a technical project manager should provide specific technology (software, hardware, and networks) he or she used to manage a project.

During the interview process, a simulation can provide a platform for the project manager candidate to demonstrate his or her actions to manage a project. Kar and Mitra (2015) suggested a behavioral questioning technique can help the project manager candidate show how he or she would react to different situations during the execution of the project. Another technique is to present the project manager candidate a simulation of a realistic project, allowing the candidate to present his or her actions to the process of running the project and the handling of risks or other project issues that can occur (Kira & Mitra, 2015). Oostrom, Mechers, Ingold, and Kleinmann (2016) investigated the use of simulation in the interviewing process. Oostrom et al. concluded simulation could be useful for the candidate to demonstrate his or her ability to resolve job tasks. The researchers were unable to measure the behavioral intentions of the candidate in the simulation; however, findings suggested how the candidate behaved during the simulation would be the same on the job.

Certified Project Manager

A person will consider a project management certification for a variety of reasons. Blomquist, Farashah, and Thomas (2018) suggested a person pursuing a project management certification is a voluntary action. Blomquist et al. questioned if the pursuit of becoming certified in project management was to become more knowledgeable in the profession (being good), add the accomplishment to a resume (looking good), or a personal and professional satisfaction (feeling good). Blomquist et al. surveyed 435 participants in 2004 and 598 in 2014. Blomquist et al. concluded participants of 2004 pursued certification for knowledge (being good) and professional satisfaction (feeling good) because motivated by intrinsic rewards. Participants in 2014 sought the certification for all three outcomes: being good, feeling good, and looking good; however, motivation factors are non-existent (Blomquist et al., 2018). A project manager will need to evaluate if the money invested in certification will provide the knowledge necessary to perform the job successfully.

A certification in project management standards proves a candidate understands the knowledge to run a project; however, the certification a requirement for potential candidates. Joseph and Marnewick (2018) investigated if project managers who are PMP or PRINCE2 certified to perform better than those who do not have certifications in project management. Joseph and Marnewick conducted a quantitative study, surveying 1731 participants who are information technology project managers in South Africa. Joseph and Marnewick concluded neither certification (PMP or PRINCE2) guaranteed the project manager would ensure project success or improve project performance. Saade, Dong, and Wan (2015) conducted a mixed methods study analyzing critical success factors of project success defined in the context of the United Nations. The sample population included 200 participants of a UN organization trained in PRINCE2 (Saade et al., 2015). Factors included PMP or PRINCE2 certified or trained (Saade et al., 2015). The data results depicted 6% of the participants were PMP certified and 32% were PRINCE2 certified (Saade et al.,

2015). Saade et al. concluded a certification of PMP or PRINCE2 was not relevant to a project manager delivering project success. Communication and interpersonal skills with stakeholders, the team, customers, and others involved in the project proved more critical (Saade et al., 2015). Although the certification confirms the candidate understands project management standards, the certification does not ensure project success.

Artificial Intelligence for Recruiting

Receiving a plethora of job applications can become overwhelming for the hiring manager. Some companies have developed human resources information systems or applicant tracking systems to use artificial intelligence (AI) to eliminate candidates that do not meet the required skills (Upadhyay & Khandelwal, 2018). AI is the gathering of big data by a computer program that will develop algorithms to interpret and learn from the historical data (Haenlein & Kaplan, 2019). Tambe, Cappelli, and Yakubovich (2019) provided challenges hiring managers need to be aware of before deciding to use AI. Human resource data is complex (Tambe et al., 2019). A common human resource algorithm could interpret historical data based on gender and performance (Tambe et al., 2019). Amazon's human resources used AI that created a similar algorithm for hiring, concluding white men as the best performers; therefore, the best candidates for job openings (Meyer, 2018). The algorithm disqualified women for the same job opportunities (Meyer, 2018). Tambe et al. concluded AI is a process that needs time to perfect before using AI algorithms to interpret data for hiring purposes. The use of AI creates concerns by the candidates of fairness; therefore, questioning ethical and other legal constraints (Tambe et al., 2019). Tambe et al. stressed the importance of understanding the AI algorithms and data results to ensure no legal repercussions. Although AI can eliminate manual work of reviewing a plethora of candidates for a job opening, the hiring manager must ensure the algorithm is accurate and fair.

Discussion

As the job market continues to increase with job opportunities (U.S. BLS, 2020), company leaders need project managers (PMI, 2020b). Determining the appropriate required skills on a job posting will ensure the company leader is hiring the best person for the project management position. A project manager must have knowledge and skills about managing projects, proven performance of managing projects, and personal skills to communicate effectively with the project team, stakeholders, business leaders, customers, and vendors (PMI, 2017a). A project is temporary with an end date (PMI, 2017a); therefore, the business leader must determine the time frame of the position or if the candidate will work on additional future projects.

Several studies were analyzed to determine what skills a project manager would need to deliver project success. A project manager can pursue PMP, CAPM (PMI, 2020b), IPMA (IPMA, 2020b), or PRINCE2 (Axelos, n.d.) certification to prove he or she knows how to manage projects. Ahsan et al. (2013) concluded certification does not ensure project success; however, Blomquist et al. (2018) suggested earning a certification provides a sense of personal and professional accomplishment. Project management methodologies (Kanban, Scrum, Lean, Waterfall, and Agile) provide an organized work structure of project management processes, developing repetitive tasks or the opportunity to improve the tasks (Pace, 2019). Pace (2019) acknowledged project management methodologies do not ensure project success; however, he found the adaptation, maturation, or tailoring of the project management processes could. Zwikael and Meredith (2017) indicated a lack of consistency in project management terms among companies. A hiring manager will want to ensure to use the correct terminology in a job posting attract the appropriate candidates. Hoxha and McMahan (2019) determined the age of a project manager does not impact project success.

Hiring managers use simulations in an interview, allowing the candidate to demonstrate the action taken to do the job. Kar and Mitra (2015) recommended simulations for interviewing project managers to examine interpersonal skills and how the candidate would react to project risks. Oostrom et al. (2016) confirmed simulation provides a platform for candidates to demonstrate how he or she would act on the job.

Hiring managers may receive overwhelming responses to a job posting. Company leaders use AI to process big data, including candidate information (Upadhyay & Khandelwal, 2018). AI algorithms need thorough tested to ensure the processing of data is accurate and fair that could otherwise result in legal issues (Tambe et al., 2019).

Conclusion

A project manager should be assigned to a project immediately, preferably during the creation of the project charter. The hiring manager and business leader must first understand what role the project manager will fulfill: project manager, project expeditor, or project coordinator to determine the required skill set needed to list in the job posting. Next, the length of the position needs to be determined: permanent or temporary. If temporary, the hiring manager should consider the time necessary to complete the project and if the new hire would be a temporary employee or consultant. Determining project success will help the hiring manager identify skills required; keeping in mind age is not a factor. Many company leaders and employees use terminology that pertains to unique business strategies and processes. The hiring manager will need to translate these unique terms to standard terminology used in project management, preferably the PMBOK® Guide by the PMI. Listing a required skillset using PMBOK Guide terminology could help eliminate people applying for the position that does not meet these qualifications. The hiring manager should also consider what knowledge areas are needed to complete a project. Communication and interpersonal skills were proven more important than certification. A person can seek a PMP, CAPM, IPMA, or PRICE2 certification for personal and professional accomplishments. Candidates could demonstrate their actions of running a project in a simulation. Although AI continues to be accessible for identifying candidates that meet the required skills, the hiring manager must ensure the AI algorithms are accurate and will not create unethical decisions. Hiring managers and business leaders should consider the refractive thinking approach to develop strategies to ensure hiring the perfect project manager.

THOUGHTS FROM THE ACADEMIC ENTREPRENEUR

The Problem to be Solved:
- What strategies are available to ensure the hiring manager and/or business leader is hiring the perfect project manager.

The Goals:
- Understanding the strategies to hire a project manager that fits the business needs will lead to project success.

The Questions to Ask:
- What hiring strategies are required to hire the perfect project manager to guarantee project success?
- Is the experience of the project manager an advantage to project success?
- Are one or more certifications, such as PMP, CAPM, IPMA, or PRINCE2 an advantage to project success?
- Will emerging technologies, such as artificial intelligence a tool to guarantee hiring the perfect project manager?

Today's Business Application:
- The expected role, timeframe of project, definition of project success, and knowledge areas required to complete the project will help the hiring manager create a list of required skill sets the candidate must have to fill the position.
- Age and certification should not deter a person's application for the position.
- Communication and interpersonal skills are important; therefore, a simulation could prove beneficial in an interview.
- AI should not be used in eliminate candidates unless thoroughly tested.

REFERENCES

Ahsan, K., Ho, M., & Khan, S. (2013). Recruiting project managers: A comparative analysis of competencies and recruitment signals from job advertisements. *Project Management Journal, 44*(5), 36-54. doi:10.1002/pmi.21366

Axelos. (n.d.). *PRINCE2 Agile – Project management.* Retrieved from https://www.axelos.com/best-practice-solutions/prince2-agile

Blomquist, T., Farashah, A. D., & Thomas, J. (2018). Feeling good, being good and looking good: Motivations for, and benefits from, project management certification. *International Journal of Project Management, 36*, 498-511. doi:10.1016/j.iporman.2017.11.006

Haenlein, M., & Kaplan, A. (2019). A brief history of artificial intelligence: On the past, present, and future of artificial intelligence. *California Management Review, 61*(4), 5-14. doi:10.1177/0008125619864925

Hoxha, L., & McMahan, C. (2018). Does a project manager's work experience help project success? *International Journal of Construction Project Management, 10*(2). 155-172. Retrieved from https://www.journals.elseview.com/international-journal-of-project-management

Hoxha, L., & McMahan, C. (2019). The influence of project manager's age on project success. *Journal of Engineering, Project, and Production Management, 9*(1). 12-19. doi:10.2478/jeppm-2019-0003

IPMA. (2020a). *About us.* Retrieved from https://www.ipma.world/about-us

IPMA. (2020b). *Building bridges worldwide between people and competences.* Retrieved from https://www.ipma.world/assets/IPMA_Main_Brochure_2017_ENG_screen.pdf

Joseph, N., & Marnewick, C. (2018). Investing in project management certification: Do organisations get their money's worth. *Information Technology and Management, 19*(1). doi:10.1007/s10799-017-0275-y

Kar, N., & Mitra, S. (2015). Recruiting a project manager: A hiring manager's perspective. *International Journal of Information Technology Project Management, 6*(1), 54-65. doi:10.4018/ijitpm.201510103

Leonard, E. (2019). So, you didn't get the job. *Reference & User Services Quarterly, 58*(3), 134-136. doi:10.5860/rusq.58.3.7038

Meyer, D. (2018). Amazon reportedly killed an AI recruitment system because it couldn't stop the tool from discriminating against women. *Fortune.* Retrieved from https://www.fortune.com/2018/10/10/amazon-ai-recruitement-bias-women-sexist

Millhollan, C., & Kaarst-Brown, M. (2016). Lessons for IT project manager efficacy: A review of the literature associated with project success. *Project Management Journal, 47*(5), 89-106. Retrieved from https://www/pmi.org/PMJ

Oostrom, J. K., Mechers, K. G., Ingold, P. V., & Kleinmann, M. (2016). Why do situational interviews predict performance? Is it saying how you would behave knowing how you should behave? *Journal of Business & Psychology, 31*(2), 279-291. doi:10.1007/s10869-015-9410-0

Pace, M. (2019). A correlational study on project management methodology and project success. *Journal of Engineering, Project, and Production Management, 9*(2), 56-65. doi:10.2478/jeppm-2019-0007

Project Management Institute (PMI). (2017a). *A guide to project management body of knowledge: PMBOK guide* (6th ed.). Newtown Square, PA: Project Management Institute.

Project Management Institute (PMI). (2017b). *Project management job growth and talent gap 2017-2027.* Retrieved from https://www.pmi.org/-/media/pmi/documents/public/pdf/learning/job-growth-report.pdf

Project Management Institute (PMI). (2020a). *About us.* Retrieved from https://www.pmi.org/about

Project Management Institute (PMI). (2020b). *Certifications.* Retrieved from https://www.pmi.org/certifications

Saade, R. G., Dong, H., & Wan, J. (2015). Factors of project manager success. *Interdisciplinary Journal of Information, 10*, 63-80. doi:10.28945/2265

Tambe, P., Cappelli, P., & Yakubovich, V. (2019). Artificial intelligence in human resources management: Challenges and a path forward. *California Management Review, 61*(4), 15-42. doi:10.1177/0008125619867910

Upadhyay, A. K., & Khandelwal, K. (2018). Applying artificial intelligence: Implications for recruitment. *Strategic HR Review, 17*(5), 255-258. doi:10.1108/SHR-07-2018-0051

U.S. Bureau of Labor Statistics (BLS). (2020). *Job openings and labor turnover: December 2019.* Retrieved from https://www.bls.gov/news.release/pdf/jolts.pdfhow

Zwikael, O., & Meredith, J. R. (2017). Who's who in the project zoo?: The ten core project roles. *International Journal of Operations & Production Management, 38*, 474-492. doi:10.1108/IJOPM-05-2017-0274

About the Author...

Dr. Natalie Casale resides in Monmouth County, New Jersey. Dr. Natalie holds several accredited degrees: a Bachelor of Science (BS) in Information Technology from Kean University, a Master of Business Administration (MBA) in Accounting from Monmouth University, and a Doctorate of Management (DM) in Organizational Leadership from the University of Phoenix School of Advanced Studies. Dr. Natalie is a part-time faculty with the University of Phoenix and Walden University. Dr. Natalie serves as a dissertation chair and committee member.

Dr. Natalie is a member of the University of Phoenix Lambda Sigma Chapter of the International Business Honor Society, Delta Mu Delta (DMD). Dr. Natalie is a volunteer National and New Jersey State District Leader of the Humane Society of the United States (HSUS) and recognized community leader in animal welfare. Dr. Natalie enjoys taking walks with her four dogs, problem solving, writing, and helping others, such as educating young adults in science, technology, engineering, and mathematics (STEM). In her spare time, she builds robots, including a cat named STEM.

To reach Dr. Natalie Casale, please visit her **website: http://www.nataliecasale.com** or **e-mail: nataliecasale@icloud.com**

CHAPTER 9

Project Management: The Stark Choice—Projectize or Stagnate

Dr. Deji West

The objective of the West (2020) study was to highlight the infancy of project management in emerging economies and the challenges confronting project management in Nigeria. Project management, as widely practiced across the globe, has its uniqueness in different countries, including Nigeria. Consistently, business growth has been sub-optimal in Nigeria despite the opportunities and the human resource (HR) capabilities. Largely, this level of performance is because of systemic weaknesses and emerging matters including inadequate project delivery skills and / or culture combined with a resulting lack of adherence to standards, increasing migration of skilled labor, and experienced project delivery personnel to the United Kingdom, United States, and Canada. There is an inadequate response on the part of government and businesses to respond to skills shortage (now and in the future) by introducing mitigations to combat skill migration practically. Furthermore, there is lukewarm or a severely limited appetite on the part of businesses to leverage the bandwidth infrastructure among other things while mitigating infrastructure deficiencies (housing, transport, and power) to seize on remote working at a sufficient scale to change the way people work for the better. The purpose of this writing is to apply the refractive thinking approach to explore the possible influence of using project-based work to support business growth in emerging markets in Africa for business sustainability and growth.

Underlying Problem

Small- and medium-sized enterprise businesses in Africa fail to adopt innovative work practices (Alam, Adeyinka, & Wiesner, 2019). Breeding innovative capability in the academic curriculum and other project practices are tools required to mitigate the influence of skill migration of the youthful demographics needed to realize the Africa promise or the global war for talent. Innovative work practices in this case refer to the purposeful and intentional adoption of a fit-for-purpose project-based working model that exploits gains in bandwidth and availability of remote working tools. This mitigates the impact of poor infrastructure (transport particularly and power) to create a sustainable, attractive and effective remote working channel for the brilliant and committed workforce. The impact is an engaged and thriving business ecosystem.

Additionally, such a remote working model could raise standards of work by allowing experienced practitioners abroad to support talent still in Africa (Nigeria). The current way of working *(fixed contracts, minimal virtual working, and hierarchical organization)* cannot deliver optimal results for businesses in the contemporary business environment in Nigeria (Alam et al., 2019). The goal of a previous study by Daniel and Pasquire (2019) was to explore the strategies that project managers had used in a project-based environment in retaining talents. The need to have an in-depth understanding of the strategy of retaining talent is to help businesses deal optimally with the disruption introduced by global mobility of talent. Some of the strategies used by project managers may provide education to business leaders regarding the efficacy of projectized organizations to be agile and responsive to business changes through systemic adaptation and evolution of a projectized approach for business growth and relevance. The implications for social change include employment sustainability, better standards of living, job creation, and a more productive economy in Nigeria.

Project Management in Retrospect

A *project* is a temporary event with a defined beginning and end in time, with a defined scope and resources (Jara, Babb, & Flohr, 2019). A project is a unique event, not a routine operation, but a specific set of operations designed to accomplish a singular goal (Jara et al., 2019). A project team comprises of different people and usually do not work together; sometimes, they work from different organizations and across multiple geographies (Jara et al., 2019). Project management is the application of knowledge, skills, tools, and techniques to project activities to meet the project requirement (Jara et al., 2019). The project management framework serves as an agreed best practice for project coordination across the world (Jara et al., 2019).

Impact of Brain Drain on Project Management

The challenges confronting project management practice include the understanding that project management is a unique methodology for project delivery and business success. The project manager should be aware of both international and domestic influences when executing the project management functions (Kligaard & Gottlieb, 2019). Some of these challenges are (a) cultural differences, (b) political factors, (c) legal factors, (d) economic factors, and (e) technological factors (Jara et al., 2019). These factors are important because a project manager needs to understand factors that contribute to the success and failure in project delivery.

Cultural Differences

Countries have their different languages, etiquettes, and practices that the project manager must abide by to cope with the project management environment (Akanni, Oke, & Akpomiemie, 2015). In an international project where language becomes a barrier, the need for language interpreter may become necessary, which would also come with a cost. The inability to understand the host community language affects the project delivery time as a result of a delay in interpretation from human resources (Ligaard & Gottlieb, 2019). The cultural practice, such as prayer time for the Muslims, may be strange to non-Muslims who may not understand why workers will take five times a day to observe prayers. The ability of the project manager to have cross-cultural skills in managing cultural differences may improve the project management practice (Akanni et al., 2015; Wilbosono, Govindaraju, Irianto, & Sudirman, 2019). A good knowledge of country dynamics will better equip the project manager to succeed in the project execution. A project manager may understand several cultures and languages, but the use of interpreters or studying the culture of the people is sustainable.

Political Factors

In the investigation of challenges to project management to more than 20 participants, political risk ranked first. In Nigeria, where the political cycle is every 4 years, companies resolved to have 4 year strategic plans, rather than a long-term business strategy to cope with the political cycles in Nigeria (Henderson, Stackman, & Lindekilde, 2018). The reasons for the 4 years' business plan include political instability, ethnic, and communal clashes that occur during the elections in Nigeria. At the international stage, political wills and caprices influence project management.

As a result of both international and domestic political instability, projects get postponed creating room for political stability (Henderson et al., 2018). Project managers should adapt to the practice of the community they operate to cope with the complete political activities that may occur during project execution.

Legal Factors

One threat to doing business globally is dealing with vast differences in legal and regulatory environments. The United States, for example, has an established set of laws and regulations that provide direction to businesses operating within its borders (Henderson et al., 2018). The absence of a global legal system for business law created a gap in establishing a framework for practice for project management practice (Kligaard & Golttlieb, 2019). For example, contract provisions and copyright protection are differently treated in different countries (Sarooghi, Libaers, & Burkemper, 2015). Companies doing international business often face many inconsistent laws and regulations. In Nigeria, the legal environment of business registration and ownership contributes significantly to why businesses could be constrained from expanding in Nigeria or otherwise (Sarooghi et al., 2015). And this is important because projects are increasingly being delivered within a global context (perhaps with international funding with strict contractual conditions); hence it is clear for project collaborators to be realistic about the impact of the legal environment on their projects and position realistically for success in the appropriate context.

Economic Factors

The economic world provides a framework for such elements as demand, supply, employment to unemployment ratio, inflation, the standard of living, competition, and sustainability (Kumar & Thakkar, 2017). The exchange rate of a country may affect projects which could be a result of other factors such as the balance of trade disparity. In 2016, the exchange rate increased from $1: ₦160 to $1: ₦360 (Arize, Kalu, Okoyeuzu, & Malindretos, 2019). During this period, Nigeria remained a volatile, uncertain, complex, and ambiguous (VUCA) country or environment for doing business (Arize et al., 2019). Many projects could not be completed as a result of economic instability; some were left at the planning stage, while some that were executed were also not commissioned as the sponsors were out of business because of the root cause of insolvency or inability to attract the foreign products that form the bedrock of their business (Arize et al., 2019). Project teams working in this context should plan for such risks and have mitigation plans from the onset. A deliberate attempt is required to plan to engage proactively in understanding and considering economic contexts during project implementation. Economic factors such as the demand and supply of labor, the stability in the exchange rate of a country, and the ease of doing business in a country can influence the success or failure of projects in that country.

Business and social impact. The findings from the West (2020) study are significant to project management practitioners who may use the experiences of project managers to improve their skills. Daniel and Pasquire (2019) mentioned the significance of the Project Management Body of Knowledge (PMBOK®) to include the updating of the curriculum as regards Nigeria's experiences on project management. The information provided serves as a lesson learned in the PMBOK. Arize et al. (2019) found out that project management is an iterative process that needs detailed appraisal of the project, which serves as a pattern in the subsequent project.

Examples of Issues

Projectized organization. The Former Managing Director (MD), Nigeria Inter-Bank Settlement System (NIBSS), implemented a transformational agenda during his 15-year tenure. NIBSS includes the primary responsibility for development of the financial industry's wide payment and settlement processes in Nigeria. When one arrived at a bank, crediting a checking account would take 3 weeks to get value for a check (Daniel & Pasquire, 2019). As a result, the populace of Nigeria preferred to do transactions with cash because of the delay in receiving the value of money in a bank account. One noticed a general apathy by the banks regarding how the central payments system could be of value to the end-user, the bank's customers. The MD decided to projectized the NIBBS organization and moved the banking industry from manual processes to digital transformation. The banks had grown accustomed to the status quo and rejected suggestions for change. The MD tactically deployed into banks that cooperated with adopting new processes thus giving them a head start of the benefits derived from the change. This compelled a quick buy in by all participants.

The NIBSS organization resolved into using teams with project managers to manage specific and timely deliverables (Umar, Ado, & Ayuba, 2019). Umar et al. (2019) found out that even the biggest detractors providing formidable resistance to change eventually became followers as the changes occurred in the banking industry in Nigeria. By the time he left office, the former MD could boast of creating the instant payment system into the country, where one can make a payment on a mobile phone with an 8 seconds delivery time (Umar et al., 2019; Wibisono et al., 2019). The NIBSS instant payment derived its early adoption and industry wide success from a subtle but highly effective strategy. In the past, NIBSS would wait until the other banks were ready, but there was a heavy cluster of narrow commercial protectionism which could derail the project. Consequently, NIBBS advertised in national dailies that all banks could initiate and receive a NIBSS instant transfer. This process turned out to be the *magic wand* for the success of this pivotal industry wide electronic payments system. All the banks immediately adopted the Instant Pay system. This MD of NIBSS in Nigeria demonstrated the relevance of using project management tools in repositioning an organization. Such a case-study confirms that project management techniques when properly introduced with the right level of sponsorship can be an enabler for business and be a super tool for transformation.

Migration of project managers from Nigeria. The migration of talented employees and employable graduates from Nigeria to other countries has influenced the low quality of project management execution in Nigeria. In the fall of 2018, a young professional received a much anticipated *golden email*, which was a request to submit his family's international passports for stamping, following the approval of their seven-month-long *Express Entry* application to relocate to Canada (Enete, Obi, Ozor, & Nma, 2016). This story is cited to show how the clamor for emigration is impacting the business environment in Nigeria. The *golden email* represents the final stage where an applicant gets the green signal to emigrate to *greener pastures*.

In this case, the relocation would inevitably impact a sizeable project he was managing as a Business Development Manager for an Oil and Gas and Power Generation servicing company. This professional with 10 years of experience, is a qualified certified engineer in Nigeria and a graduate of engineering with a master's degree in information technology both from U.K. universities. He has a family of four; his wife and two children. He had commenced a project worth $1.7m that involved Custody Transfer for three power generation plants (Enete et al., 2016). This project's timeline extended to 27 weeks. He had carefully selected his team, the Engineering, Procurement and Construction (EPC), prepared the Project Management Document (Origination, Initiation, Planning, Execution, Monitoring & Control and Closing), organized the Factory Acceptance Test (FAT), HSE compliance, Financial Budgeting, finalized all dealing with the banks regarding Advanced Payment Guarantee and Payment Bond, and started receiving various devices from Europe in phases.

The project manager mobilized his team to the project site while he and his Business Development Specialist (BDS) continued the daily management of the business. A date had already been fixed for site visits to inspect the first phase of execution and to have a project meeting with the client. The decision to travel from Nigeria to Canada in December 2019 created a gap in the project being managed prior to his decision to relocate from one country to another. Because of time-consuming preparations that were needed, he considered managing the project from Canada. Managing the project was affected by time difference and the nature of the project which required technical inspections, the value of the Nigerian Naira to Canadian Dollar and the unforeseen settling process in a new country with a family of four; and he regrettably had to hand-over the project being quite confident that the project will be successful (Enete et al., 2016).

Training timeframe. In Nigeria, the importance of project management certifications like PRojects IN Controlled Environments (PRINCE2) or Project Management Professional (PMP) is notable among employers (Carliners et al., 2015). PRINCE2 is a Project Management method which originated from the UK OGC (Office of Government Commerce). The world recognizes PRINCE2 because of its control of change from initiation to closure (Carliner et al., 2015). PMP from the Project Management

Institute (PMI) uses the PMBOK as a non-prescriptive guide from project conception to successful implementation / delivery across different industries. PRINCE2 and PMP qualifications are the minimum standards required to become a project management practitioner in Nigeria (Carliner et al., 2015). Project managers without quality certification in project management provides some evidence to why projects are abandoned and uncompleted by these so-called managers (Carliner et., al, 2015).

Uncompleted projects. Another phenomenon prevalent in Nigeria is uncompleted projects (Daniel & Pasquire, 2019). In 1995, the architect of a building in the capital city of Abuja, received recognition for a building based on approved architectural drawings as developed by a software that was being deployed for the first time by the architectural firm. The project personnel who should have performed impact analysis and pre-construction Front-End Engineering Design (FEED) were missing. Globally, project managers get recognition for building a state-of-the-art or one-of-its-kind, or entirely new technology is used, but project risk is expected to be high. The risk of uncompleted projects could influence project management practice in Abuja and Lagos. The incidence of shortcuts in the practice in Nigeria is alarming and costly. The major factors responsible for project delays and abandonment are poor planning, lackluster quality assurance, weak project control and sheer irresponsibility (Carliner et al., 2015).

Conclusion

If Nigeria is to move forward and benefit from the use of project management, the buy-in of the leaders to develop and deploy project-based work skills across different organizations is required. To enhance the delivery of business benefits in an emerging projectized economy, the project manager should adopt up to date project methods. Resourcing the right person may be difficult as there is a general outflow of skilled labor out of the country to Canada. Leaders should look for ways to augment project delivery skills with new ways of working to engage in global talent effectively. For instance, leaders could employ the right-fit persons to work remotely or virtually. Ensuring a best practice project management may enhance innovation across businesses, delivering sustainable business growth and economic improvement in the country. In this writing, I presented the underlying problems confronting project management in Nigeria. I reviewed the impact of brain drain on project management; using cultural differences, political factors, legal factors, economic factors, and the business and social impact to provide refractive thinking on project management. I also presented a case of how the MD rejuvenated the check clearing system from its limbo using the NIBSS technology. In my dissertation on succession planning in family businesses, recommendations included that future research would build on my study to have a wider view on succession planning. Introducing succession planning to the project management practice may further improve the practice in Nigeria's project ecosystem (West, 2019).

THOUGHTS FROM THE ACADEMIC ENTREPRENEUR

The Problem to be Solved:

- Workforce migration away from emerging markets (such as those in Africa) pose a threat to business productivity and adequate economic growth.
- Traditional working ways in the face of limited infrastructure. Cultural limitations and impact of globalization reduce productivity / business results.

The Goals:

- To be proactive, as well as responsive to the above challenges, introduce policies to mitigate the impact of project failure in emerging economies.

The Questions to Ask:

- How can an organization prepare for loss of key personnel especially to migration?
- How do you overcome resistance to advocacy for project management?

Today's Business Application:

- The paper provides information of challenges in the project management environment. Leaders should use the information to mitigate against or prepare for the challenges listed.
- Leaders should consider employing services of migrated key personnel on a virtual or remote basis.

REFERENCES

Akanni, P. O., Oke, A. E., & Akpomiemie, O. A. (2015). Impact of environmental factors on building project performance in Delta State, Nigeria. *HBRC Journal, 11*(1), 91-97.doi: 10.1016/j.hbrcj.2014.02.010

Alam, K., Adeyinka, A. A., & Wiesner, R. (2019). Smaller businesses and e-innovation. A winning combination in Australia. *Journal of Business Strategy, 52*, 42-71.doi:10.1108/JBS-11-2018-0186

Arize, A. C., Kalu, E. U., Okoyeuzu, C., & Malindretos, J. (2019). Exchange rate and long-run price relationship in 19 selected European and LDCS. *Journal of Financial Economic Policy, 24*, 111-171. doi:10.1108/JFEP-08-2018-0117

Carliner, S., Castonguay, C., Sheepy, E., Ribeiro, O., Sabri, H., Saylor, C., & Valle, A. (2015). The job of a performance consultant. A qualitative content analysis of job description. *European Journal of Training and Development, 39*, 458-483. doi:10.1108/EJTD-01-2015-0006

Daniel, E. I., & Pasquire, C. (2019). Creating social value within the delivery of construction projects. The role of lean approach. *Engineering Construction and Architectural Management, 25*, 1105-1128. doi:10.1108/ECAM-06-2017-0096/full/html

Enete, A. A., Obi, J. N., Ozor, N., & Mba, C. L. (2016). Socioeconomic assessment of flooding among farm households in Anambra state, Nigeria. *International Journal of Climate Change Strategies & Management, 8*, 96-111. doi:10.1108/IJOCSM-07-2014-0084

Henderson, L. S., Stackman, R. W., & Lindekilde, R. (2018). Why cultural intelligence matters on global project teams. *International Journal of Project Management, 36*, 954-967. doi:10.1016/j.ijproman.2018.06.001

Jara, E. V., Babb, J. W., & Flohr, T. M. (2019). Status and scope of project management in the hospitality industry. *International Hospitality Review, 33*, 142-149. doi:10.1108/IHR-09-2019-0016

Kligaard, A., Gottlieb, S. (2019). Strategizing and project management in construction projects. An exploratory literature review. *Emerald Reach Proceedings Series, 2*, 253-258. doi:10.1108/S2516285320190000002040

Kumar, S., Thakkar, J. J. (2017). Schedule and cost overrun analysis for R&D projects using ANP and system dynamics. *International Journal of Quality & Reliability Management, 34*, 1551-1567. doi:10.1108/IJQRM-04-2016-0050

Morris, P. W. (2012). Cleland and King. Project management and the systems approach. *International Journal of Managing Project in Business, 5*, 634-642. doi:10.1108/17538371211268951

Sarooghi, H., Libaers, D., & Burkemper, A. (2015). Examining the relationship between creativity and innovation: A meta-analysis of organizational, cultural, and environmental factors. *Journal of business venturing, 30*, 714-731. doi:10.1016/j.jbusvent.2014.12.003

Umar, U. H., Ado, M. B., & Ayuba, H. (2019). Is religion an impediment to Nigeria's financial inclusion targets by the year 2020? *Qualitative Research in Financial Markets, 5*, 1756-4179. doi:10.1108/QREM-01-2019-0010

Wibisono, Y. Y., Govindaraju, R., Irianto, D., & Sudirman, I. (2019). Managing differences, interaction and partnership quality in global inter-firm relationships. *International Journal of Managing Projects in Business, 12*, 730-754. doi:10.1108/IJMPB-04-2018-0074

West, A. (2019). Succession planning in family-owned businesses in Nigeria. Available at http://scholarworks.waldenu.edu/dissertations/7093

About the Author...

Dr. Deji West resides in Lagos, Nigeria. He is currently CEO for Upstream and Mining in the Petrolex Group, a Nigerian independent oil & gas company. He also acts as the Group CFO for the wider conglomerate. Dr West completed his Doctorate in Business Administration at Walden University. He has a Master's in Business Administration and a Bachelor's of Science in Civil Engineering, both obtained from City University, London U.K.

He has been in business for over three decades with an in-depth knowledge of finance, commerce, project management and accounting from working in several industries which include Banking, Manufacturing, Oil, & Gas and more. He has worked in Nigeria, UK, Europe, India, Singapore, Japan and the US. Dr West is a Public speaker, MC and facilitator with an incredible passion to teach. He is a past president of the Project Management Institute (PMI) in Nigeria.

In his spare time, he is a member of faculty at the Nehemiah Leadership Institute and lectures in Leadership, Business, Management, and Accounting.

To reach Dr. Deji West, please visit him at his **website: www.dejiwest.org** or **e-mail: dw@dejiwest.org**

CHAPTER 10

The Project Management—Impact of Educational Curriculum Design

Dr. Amy Yoder, Dr. Yvonne Gonzalez, Dr. Teresa Sanders, & Dr. Cheryl Lentz

The idea of project management (PM) is a business concept referring to a strategic plan to bring all aspects of a project to completion. In academia, the equivalent would be curriculum design. The challenge of the concept of project management is the approach and perception among industries, yet the fundamentals of project management remain the same. Shakespeare stated in Romeo and Juliet, "A rose by any other name is still a rose." The name attached to a concept is not as important as understanding the actual concept. The goal of this writing is to examine these fundamentals and their impact on the educational process of curriculum design and their influence on the achievement of programmatic learning objectives.

The question of importance for educators is: Are the students learning what the educators intended to teach? Will students receive a sound education to prepare them for what they will face in society personally and professionally?

Project management of educational curriculum design provides the tools for analysis through refractive thinking. This chapter focuses on five groups of project management processes including initiating, planning, executing, monitoring and controlling, and closing (Project Management Institute [PMI], 2020). The Project Management Institute (PMI) defined project management as "the application of knowledge, skills, tools, and techniques to project activities to meet the project requirements" (PMI, 2020, para. 5). While in academia,

> Curriculum design is a term used to describe the purposeful, deliberate, and systematic organization of curriculum (instructional blocks) within a class or course. In other words, it is a way for teachers to plan instruction. When teachers design curriculum, they identify what will be done, who will do it, and what schedule to follow. (Sweitzer, 2019, para. 1)

Through our writing, we will demonstrate the similarity of these two approaches as related to effective project design and the ability of the project to net the desired outcomes as expected in project management in any profession.

Curriculum Design

In 1983, the National Commission on Excellence in Education reported the United States lacked a competitive edge in educational achievement. Sepnafski (2018) expressed that the U.S. educational system continues to suffer an identity crisis. The identity crisis in the educational system raises questions about what students should be learning, how student success is defined, how student progress is measured, and how to know if and when project goals have been met.

Effectiveness of project management relating to curriculum design is necessary in 21st century education. What are educators doing to prepare students to compete in a global economy? The ineffectiveness of curriculum design, and lack of student achievement as a result, is not a new occurrence. Curriculum design, if managed effectively, can decrease retention and dropout rates (National Center for Education Statistics [NCES], 2016), narrow the persistent achievement gap in K-12 education (Robinson,

2018), and decrease the need for remedial courses in post-secondary education (Douglas-Gabriel, 2016).

Educational curriculum was initially developed in adherence to a one size fits all design (Godinho, Woolley, Scholes, & Sutton, 2017; Reynolds, Byrne, Campbell, & Spritz, 2019; Wilkins, 2018). Students are struggling academically with a one size fits all curriculum design. Student populations are diverse socially, academically, linguistically, culturally, and in many other ways. A one size fits all approach to curriculum design does not address the needs of a widely diverse student population.

Stakeholders need to consider project management, as it relates to curriculum design within education, as opportunities to explore potential biases that may hinder culturally diverse student populations (Coppus, 2018; Merritt, 2018). Lindsey, Robins, and Terrell (2019) believed culture evolves into more than ethnic or racial differences, including physical ability, faith, language, age, gender, and sexual orientation. Kuh, LeeKeenan, Given, and Beneke (2016) expressed that many classrooms have a cultural blindness or cultural pre-competence approach to diversity.

An anti-bias approach is necessary for academic success of diverse student populations, to include purposeful project management of curriculum design. Anti-bias education requires more than implementation of activities in the classroom, rather "a way of teaching that supports students to develop a sense of identity in a diverse society" (Kuh, LeeKeenan, Given, & Beneke, 2016, p. 58). Conyers (2019) highlighted a proposed method for students to engage in daily dialogue on examples of anti-bias work, cultural competence, and social justice. The appealing factor to Conyers' method is no additional work or special assignments on the students' already rigorous academic workload is required.

Myer v. State of Nebraska (1923) determined teachers are bound by laws that dictate what they can teach within the United States. In 2020, States continue to dictate educational standards.

In this era of accountability and ongoing push for results, teachers are limited to what they will teach, but not limited to how they will teach. In 1994, the Clinton administration made changes to the Elementary and Secondary Act of 1965, requiring States to develop standardized tests. Student progress in 21st century education is defined and measured by achievement on standardized tests (Rambo-Hernandez, Peters, & Plucker, 2019), lacking understanding of the comprehensive, multifarious and unique needs of students and schools (Gonzalez, 2014; Sanders, 2012).

Racial and class inequalities exist not because teachers and schools practice a one-size-fits-all instruction model in public education, but rather because educational policymakers fail to adapt to the dynamic needs of students (McSpadden, 2015; Superville, 2017). The challenge to policymakers is when considering the complex requirements of learners, the institutional demands for efficiency and cost-recovery, and the practice obligations of professional educators (Silver & Lentz, 2012). Students are line items in a budget—the consumer learner within the business of academia (Silver & Lentz, 2002). A system where standards were determined by states seems to have changed to a system driven by money and politics as opposed to student needs or success.

> The learner-centric focus is of enormous pertinence to use here, but we are also intrigued by the emergence of the student not only as the recipient of knowledge within the classroom, but how somewhere along this continuum, student, and faculty communication has moved toward a more transactional business approach. . . . By the time these learners reach college, their concept of responsiveness may merge with the view of service as paying customers who have a choice of where they pursue degree acquisition. This transition in thinking changes interactions with the systems, and in those who translate—and hopefully make relevant—the curriculum. (Silver & Lentz, 2002, p. 5)

How can educators or society begin to address the need of a curriculum design that meets the needs of all learners at all levels of education? For example, test anxiety is a factor with which many students struggle at different levels of education (Fergus & Limbers, 2019). Test anxiety is common among test takers (Smith, 2020). For some students, the pressure to do well on a test results in anxiety so significant that overall test performance decreases (Smith 2020), despite the fact the tester (student) has a sufficient grasp on the tested content.

Something as simple as the use of language can affect test outcomes. When considering language as part of the pursuit to match learning outcomes with academic goals (educational project management), the result was positive. Simply swapping the term *test* with a different term, such as exercise, scavenger hunt, learning opportunity, or review, the author reported student scores increased dramatically.

Words are just words until the receiver or sender gives them meaning based on personal experiences, and biases (acculturation and enculturation) (Silver & Lentz, 2012). Consequently, words can have a major impact on outcomes. Moving forward, as educators undertake curriculum design, the use of language as part of the design is certainly worthy of review.

Testing has been the traditional measure of curriculum and course objectives. However, as one would critique project management outcomes in business, so must educators determine whether results of a test (or whatever term one uses) reflects the expectation of learning the instructor intended to net. Vance (2018) reported that psychology influences the use of language. If the desired outcome is to have students learn the content intended to be taught, educators must be mindful of the psychology that may accompany curriculum design as a function of project management.

Academic Achievement in the United States

The current lackluster academic achievement of students in the nation's public schools indicates curriculum design is among a variety of components in education that requires critical review. In a perfect world, all learners would participate in a full, inclusive curriculum that is both comprehensive and rigorous. Concurrently, curriculum would be inclusive of the needs of all students. Unfortunately, not all students have been sufficiently prepared to engage in curriculum with their grade-level peers. Underprepared students are more likely to fail in school, drop-out early and encounter hardships socially and financially in their adult lives (NCES, 2017). The following data indicates that exploration of curriculum design is timely and in order.

Consider the reading performances of America's fourth graders. The NCES (2017) indicated an unacceptable three million out of four million fourth graders, a full 75% of 4th grade students in the United States cannot read proficiently (Sanders, 2012). Of the three million nonreading 4th graders, an alarming 70% of these children will face significant difficulty reading grade-level material (NCES, 2017) in class. The NCES (2017) data indicated two thirds of the trailing 70% of students will drop out of high school before graduating and will not likely be sufficiently prepared to become industrious contributors in the workplace.

Statistically, students who drop out of high school include entrance into a life of poverty, welfare, and perhaps incarceration (U.S. Department of Justice, 2015). Additionally, the American workforce may suffer a shortage of skilled workers, especially in the sciences, leaving a breach in future generation's proficiency to meet the nation's business needs (Sanders & Lentz, 2018).

An examination of fourth and eighth grade students' math performances are cause for concern as well. Math scores for America's fourth and eighth grade students improved under No

Child Left Behind in 2002, but have been stable ever since (Hansen, Mann, Valant & Quintero, 2018). In fact, 2017 eighth grade math scores were the same as they were in 2009 (Hansen et al., 2018).

There was a drop in eighth grade math scores from 2013 to 2015. Eighth grade reading scores for Black, White, and Hispanic students have been largely stagnant, showing only a slight gain in the last few years (Hansen et al., 2018). Growth in eighth grade civics is similarly dismal to achievement in eighth grade reading performances. Growth in civics scores has been slow and modest with a small increase noted in recent years (Hansen et al., 2018). Gaps between subgroups in 4th and 8th grade reading and math and 8th grade civics remain disturbingly wide (Hansen et al., 2018; Jacobsen, 2019; Sparks, 2019).

The Programme for International Student Assessment (PISA) (2015) gauges reading ability, science, and math literacy of 15-year-old students every 3 years in developed and developing countries (DeSilver, 2017). The latest PISA results from 2015, indicated the United States ranked a mediocre 38th out of 71 countries in math and 24th out of 71 countries in science (DeSilver, 2017).

The 35-member Organization for Economic Cooperation and Development (ECD) sponsors the PISA initiative (DeSilver, 2017). Among the 35 member countries of the organization, the United States ranked 30th in math and 19th in science. Ranking 30th out of 35 in math and 19th out of 35 in science should be an embarrassment to education policymakers, educators, and all related stakeholders. With so much dependent on effective curriculum, approaching curriculum development through the lens of project management may be good policy for education.

Student Achievement and Curriculum Design

Student performance and school curriculum for K-12 education is at the forefront for critiques about whether teachers adequately reach the next generation of students to prepare them to master state and national learning standards. Most of the criticism centers on the school curriculum and the instructional practices of teachers (Asempapa, 2017; Oliver & Oesterreich, 2013; O'Shea & O'Shea, 1997).

Despite education reform since *A Nation at Risk*, student achievement remains at the forefront of the public's concern (Hammer, 2003). However, while many scholars spent time examining the role of the teacher, curriculum, and instruction (Asempapa, 2017; Oliver & Oesterreich, 2013; O'Shea & O'Shea, 1997), little research includes investigation of the K-12 audience–the students.

Beginning in 2000, the population of those enrolled in K-12 schools included Generation Z students, those born between 1995-2012 (Seemiller & Grace, 2016). With the understanding that the last of the Millennials graduated from secondary schools in 2012, K-12 school leaders face the challenge of trying to create an academic environment that appeals to and fosters learning of the next generation of students. K-12 schools can no longer use a *one-size-fits-all* mentality as these K-12 schools assume the role of helping students grow academically because the beliefs, values, and behaviors of generations differ (Twenge et al., 2015; Young, 2009).

Meet Generation Z

Generation Z, otherwise known as *Gen Next*, *iGen*, *Gen I*, or the *Digital Natives* (Jain, Vatsa, & Jagani, 2014; Seemiller & Grace, 2016; Twenge, 2017)—includes those born between 1995-2012 and tend to be the children of Millennials (Igel & Urquhort, 2012; Jain et al., 2014; Seemiller & Grace, 2016). Generation Z is the first generation born into the age of technology, and, as a result, they fail to comprehend a world where technology does not exist (Seemiller & Grace, 2016). Although the media influenced the worldview of previous generations, Generation Z's worldview remains shaped by its access to technology (Seemiller & Grace, 2016). Despite Generation Z's over-reliance on technology, Igel and Urquhort (2012) described Generation Z as smarter, more self-directed, and one who possesses the ability to process information quickly. Like Igel and Urquhort, Wiedmer (2015) augmented that Generation Z possesses higher intelligence quotients or IQs, than previous generations and requires less direction when learning, mainly because of technology. The accessibility of technology continues to be the defining characteristic that separates and shapes Generation Z from previous generations, which requires K-12 schools to approach the development of curriculum differently.

Generation Z and Curriculum Development

Despite the intentional efforts of K-12 schools to foster student achievement, not every student is meeting the state and national standards as indicated by the recurrent need for educational reform (Igel & Urquhort, 2012; Zhao, 2015). Most educational reform concentrates on standardization, uniformity, data-driven practices, and outcomes (Oliver & Oesterreich, 2012; Zhao, 2015), which fails to prepare Generation Z for the technology driven world they live in. Instead, Zhao (2015) contended that school reform should stop trying to homogenize learning and aim to support the development of diverse talents, cultivate creativity, foster a global perspective while being applicable in the 21st century. Teachers should not try to standardize curriculum for

Generation Z in the same way as previous generations. Notably, Generation Z's unique characteristics should remain at the forefront as teacher's design and implement curriculum, which requires teachers to create and execute a relevant, meaningful, and relational curriculum.

Relevant. Because of the abundance of technology, Generation Z conditioned themselves to only engage in content that is immediately relevant (Seemiller & Grace, 2016). Similarly, Yoder (2020) discovered that Generation Z students tended to perceive the learning curriculum as valuable when the content was relevant and applicable to their lives. Generation Z remains inundated with vast amounts of information that they have trained themselves to only acknowledge or read material that is immediately relevant or applicable to them (Yoder, 2020; Seemiller & Grace, 2016).

Teachers must establish relevancy in their daily lessons / curriculum to activate engagement from a new generation (Vrba & Mitchell, 2019). The advancement of technology ensures that students can learn anything from anywhere and at any time, which can allow teachers to explore unique and innovative methods to make content relevant to Generation Z. Teachers can also enable students to identify ways curriculum connects outside of the classroom and be used to make a difference in their lives and communities (Yoder, 2020). At the core of project management with curriculum design requires teachers to identify the various approaches to make curriculum consequential in the lives of a Generation Z. Instead of teachers prescribing a limited exploration of content based upon standards and state assessments, teachers should personalize standards to a new generation of students that permits the development of their unique and creative talents (Zhao, 2015). By eliminating a *one size fits all* perspective of curriculum, teachers can empower students discover their potential through a curriculum that allows them to learn the skills within the standards while exploring their passions and engage in learning without the excess of standardized assessments.

Meaningful. Generation Z desires meaningful learning experiences (Yoder, 2020). With technology at their fingertips, they look for teachers to show them the why behind the curriculum they learn (Vrba, & Mitchell, 2019; Yoder, 2020). Generation Z wants engaging and interactive experiences in addition to challenging curriculum (Seemiller & Grace, 2016; Yoder, 2020). Teachers can enable students to see meaning behind what they are learning by offering choices and giving students the freedom to express their learning in various ways (Seemiller & Grace, 2016; Yoder, 2020). Teachers should not expect every student to demonstrate mastery of learning in the same way. For a new curriculum approach to become a reality, teachers must be willing to take risks and work beyond the pretexts of what previous curriculum has been. The new project management goal of education encompasses the ability of teachers to personalize curriculum design based upon the needs of students rather than focus on the same prescribed curriculum year after year. Zhao (2015) asserted that teachers should allow students to create authentic products to demonstrate mastery, which will allow them to explore personal interest within the content and build the much needed skills for the 21st century.

Relational. Although Generation Z students are technology literate, they value face-to-face interaction and collaboration (Seemiller & Grace, 2016; Yoder, 2020). Generation Z also desires a learning environment where they can express their opinions, discuss with their peers, and co-create their education experiences through multiple forms of collaboration (Seemiller & Grace, 2016 Yoder, 2020). More importantly, using technology, students can interact with others globally (Seemiller & Grace, 2016). Teachers need to facilitate opportunities for students to collaborate in a variety of ways: face-to-face, online, and even hybrid (Vrba & Mitchell, 2019). Furthermore, teachers need to abandon the mentality that learning takes place within the four walls of a classroom and engage students in learning opportunities that exist in a global community.

Conclusion

The goal of this writing was to equivocate these fundamentals of project management and education demonstrating their impact within the educational process of curriculum design and its impact through the achievement of programmatic and course learning objectives. The question of importance for education is how to provide a learner centric focus to ensure that students learn what educators intend to teach to provide a solid degree education to prepare graduates for what they will face in society personally and professionally. Project management i.e., curriculum design provides the tools for analysis through the use of refractive thinking that included the five groups of project management processes of (a) initiating, (b) planning, (c), executing, (d) monitoring and controlling, and (e) closing (PMI, 2020).

Dr. Amy Yoder, Dr. Yvonne Gonzalez, Dr. Teresa Sanders, & Dr. Cheryl Lentz

THOUGHTS FROM THE ACADEMIC ENTREPRENEUR

The Problem to be Solved:

- Curriculum design has not evolved with the needs of new generations. As a result, America's students are falling short of state, federal and international education goals.

The Goals:

- Understanding how a one size fits all approach to curriculum design is no longer conducive to K-12 students. The approach to curriculum design, standards, and assessments must reflect evolving generational characteristics.

- Advocating for a more equitable curriculum that supports awareness of socioeconomic racial and cultural diversity and related obstacles to education reform.

The Questions to Ask:

- How can educators effectively design curriculum effectively for a new generation of students? Should curriculum design be a living, evolving process?

Today's Business Application:

- Effective curriculum that reflects the needs and characteristics of the learners to be served by it could impact positively the persistent lackluster achievement of America's students.

- Educators who understand the characteristics and needs of each generation will tailor their curriculum to meet those needs by focusing on relevance, meaning, and relational components in their content area. Proactive adaptation of curriculum to meet the unique characteristics of new generations may allow educators to teach effectively the same standards as previous generations while fostering the appropriate critical thinking skills that will prepare Generation Z to enter a technology and global driven society. Educators must teach students to be successful in a world that may seem foreign to teachers themselves.

REFERENCES

Asempapa, R. (2017). How did we get here?: The path to our current K-12 mathematics education curriculum in the United States. *AURCO Journal, 23*, 1. Retrieved from http://aurco.orm

Conyers, N. (2019). The relationship between anti-bias curriculum and cultural competency among middle school students. Retrieved fromhttp://sophia.stkate.edu/maed/295

Coppus, S. A. (2018) Anti-bias curriculum. *Anti-Bias Curriculum—Research Starters Education*, 1.

DeSilver, D. (2017). U.S. academic achievement lags that of many other countries. Retrieved from https://www.pewresearch.org/fact-tank/2017/02/15/u-s-students-internationally-math-science

Douglas-Gabriel D. (2016). Remedial classes have become a hidden cost of college. *The Washington Post*. Retrieved from https://www.washingtonpost.com/news/grade-point/wp/2016/04/06/remedial-classes-have-become-a-hidden-cost-of-college/

Fergus, T. A., & Limbers, C. A. (2019). Reducing test anxiety in school settings: A controlled pilot study examining a group format delivery of the attention training technique among adolescent students. *Behavior Therapy, 50*, 803-816. https://dx.doi.org/10.1016/j.beth.2018.12.001

Godinho, S., Woolley, M., Scholes, M., & Sutton, G. (2017). Literacies for remote schools: Looking beyond a one size fits all approach. *Literacy Learning: The Middle Years, 25*(1), 28-40.

Gonzalez, Y. L. (2014). *Improving Hispanic students' performance on science standardized tests: Successful practices from four elementary campuses* (Doctoral Dissertation). Available from ProQuest Dissertations and Thesis database. (UMI No. 3583985)

Hammer, B. (2003). A nation still at risk, panel says: Two decades after publication of landmark education study, scholars find little progress. (Noteworthy News). *Black Issues in Higher Education*, (7), 10. Retrieved from https://www.questia.com/

Hansen, M., Mann., E., Valant, J., & Quintero, D. (2018). Brown Center Report on American Education: Trends in NAEP math, reading and civics scores. Retrieved from https://www.brookings.edu/research/2018-brown-center-report-on-american-education-trends-in-naep-math-reading-and-civics-scores/

Igel, C., & Urquhort, V. (2012, March). Generation Z, meet cooperative learning. *Middle School Journal, 43*(4), 16-21. http://dx.doi.org/10.2307/41432109

Jacobsen, L. (2019). NAEP Reading scores 2019: Reading scores drop for U.S. students with mixed math results. Retrieved from https://www.educationdive.com/news/naep-2019-reading-scores-drop-for-us-students-with-mixed-math-results/566090/

Jain, V., Vatsa, R., & Jagani, K. (2014). Exploring generation Z's purchase behavior towards luxury apparel: A conceptual framework. *Romanian Journal of Marketing, 2*, 18-29. Retrieved from ttps://trove.nla.gov.au/version/225063397

Kuh, L., LeeKeenan, D., Given, H., & Beneke, M. (2016). Moving beyond anti-bias activities: Supporting the development of anti-bias practices. *Young Children, 71*(1), 58-65.

Levine, A. (2010). Teacher education must respond to changes in America. *Phi Delta Kappan, 91*(6), 19–24. https://dx.doi.org/10.1177/003172171009200205

Lindsey, R. B., Robins, K. N., & Terrell, R. D. (2019). *Cultural proficiency: A manual for school leaders* (4th ed.). Thousand Oaks, CA: Corwin Press.

McSpadden, K. (2015). Public schools aren't failing. *The Charlotte Observer*. Retrieved from http://www.charlotteobserver.com/opinion/op-ed/article9499466.html.

Merritt, R. D. (2018). Ability grouping. *Ability Grouping—Research Starters Education*, 1.

Myer v. State of Nebraska, 262 U.S. 390, 402 & 403 (1923).

National Commission on Excellence in Education (NCEE). (1983). A Nation at Risk: The Imperative for Educational Reform. Retrieved from https://www2.ed.gov/pubs/NatAtRisk/risk.html

National Center for Education Statistics (NCES). (2016). *Status dropout rates*. Retrieved from https://nces.ed.gov/programs/coe/indicator coj.asp

National Center for Education Statistics (NCES). (2017). *Reading Achievement of U.S. fourth-grade students in an international context*. Retrieved from https://nces.ed.gov/pubsearch/pubsinfo.asp?pubid=2018017

Oliver, K. L., & Oesterreich, H. A. (2013). Student-centered inquiry as curriculum as a model for field-based teacher education. *Journal of Curriculum Studies, 45*, 394–417. doi:10.1080/00220272.2012.719550

O'Shea, D. J., & O'Shea, L. J. (1997). Collaboration and school reform: A twenty-first-century perspective. *Journal of Learning Disabilities, 30*, 449-462. http://dx.doi.org/10.1177/002221949703000412

Rambo-Hernandez, K. E., Peters, S. J., & Plucker, J. A. (2019). Quantifying and exploring elementary school excellence gaps across schools and time. *Journal of Advanced Academics, 30*, 383-415. https://dx.doi.org/10.1177/1932202X19864116

Reynolds, D., Byrne, L., Campbell, J., & Spritz, B. (2019). One size doesn't fit all students' perceptions of FYE approaches. *Journal of the Scholarship of Teaching & Learning, 19*(3), 105-118. Retrieved from https://dx.doi.org/10.14434/josotl.v19i2.23844

Robinson, K. J. (2018). Restructuring the Elementary and Secondary Education Act's Approach to Equity. *Minnesota Law Review, 103*, 915-998.

Sanders, T. (2012). *A qualitative exploration of barriers to parental involvement in school activities among economically disadvantaged African American families* (Doctoral dissertation). Available from ProQuest Dissertations and Theses Database.

Sanders, T., & Lentz, C. (2018). The refractive thinker® Vol XVI: Generations: Strategies for managing generations in the work force. *Chapter 10: Fundamentals of success through generations* (pp. 171–181). Grayslake, IL: The Refractive Thinker® Press.

Schweitzer, K. (2019, November 12). Curriculum design: Definition, purpose, and types. Retrieved from https://www.thoughtco.com/curriculum-design-definition-4154176

Sepnafski, K. (2018). Developing K-12 Curriculum from the Bottom-Up: Using ADR Techniques to Meet the Needs of Students. *Ohio State Journal on Dispute Resolution, 33*(2), 279-302.

Silver, G., & Lentz, C. (2012). *The consumer learner: Emerging expectations of a customer service mentality in higher education.* Las Vegas, NV: Pensiero Press.

Seemiller, C., & Grace, M. (2016). *Generation Z goes to college.* San Francisco, CA: Jossey-Bass.

Smith, K. (2020). Managing test anxiety: How to cope and perform better. Retrieved from https://www.psycom.net/managing-test-anxiety/

Sparks, S. (2019). Achievement gaps. The achievement gaps refuse to close. Retrieved from https://www.edweek.org/ew/articles/2019/04/10/achievement-gaps-1.html

Superville, D. R. (2017). Closing failing schools doesn't help most students, study finds. *Education Week.* Retrieved from https://www.edweek.org/ew/articles/2017/08/24/closing-failing-schools-doesnt-help-most-students.html

Turner, A. (2015). Generation Z. Technology and social interest. *Journal of Individual Psychology, 71*(2), 103-113. http://dx.doi.org/10.1353/jip.2015.0021

Twenge, J. M. (2017). *iGen: Why today's super-connected kids are growing up less rebellious, more tolerant, less happy, and completely unprepared for adulthood.* New York, NY: Atria Books.

U.S. Department of Justice. (2015). *Title IX of the Education Amendments of 1972.* Retrieved from https://www.justice.gov/crt/title-ix-education-amendments-1972

Vance, N. (2018). The Affective Variable. *Affective Variable—Research Starters Education*, 1.

Vrba, T., & Mitchell, K. (2019). Contemporary classroom innovation: Exploration. *Journal of Instructional Pedagogies*, 22. Retrieved from https://www.aabri.com/

Wiedmer, T. (2015). Generations do differ: Best practices in leading traditionalists, boomers, and generations X, Y, and Z. *Delta Kappa Gamma Bulletin, 82*(1), 51-58.

Wilkins, S. (2018). Unlocked Potential: Carroll School adopted a data-driven mindset to find solutions to the one-size-fits-all problem and deliver an education focused on what its students most need. *Independent School, 77*(2), 85.

Yoder, A. C. (2020). *Spiritual formation strategies for generation Z students in a secondary*

Christian school (Doctoral dissertation). Available from ProQuest Dissertations & Theses Global. (UMI No. 2307165122)

Young, K. (2009). The X, Y and Z of generations in schools. *International Journal of Learning, 16*(7), 203-215. Retrieved from https://www.ijlter.org

Zhao, Y. (2015). A world at risk: An imperative for a paradigm shift to cultivate 21st century learners. *Society, 52*(2), 129. http://dx.doi.org /10.1007/s12115-015-9872-8

About the Authors...

Dr. Amy C. Yoder resides in the historic town of Peoria, AZ and has been an educator for over 20 years with experience in public and private institutions at the secondary and collegiate levels. Dr. Yoder is a university professor on faculty with Grand Canyon University and Ashford University. Dr. Yoder also teaches dual enrollment courses at a private Christian high school in Phoenix, AZ. Dr. Yoder serves as a curriculum developer and instructional designer for various universities and online high schools and a dissertation committee member.

Awards include: ACSI Teacher of the Year, Rio Salado Faculty of the Year, and Rio Salado Outstanding Assessment Contributions.

Additional published works include her dissertation: *Spiritual Formation Strategies for Generation Z Students in a Secondary Christian School*. Dr. Yoder additionally provides professional development for staff at ACSI Christian schools on Generation Z and spiritual formation.

To reach Dr. Amy Yoder for information on Christian education or guest speaking, please **e-mail: dramycyoder@gmail.com**

Dr. Yvonne L. Gonzalez earned her doctoral degree in Educational Leadership in 2014. She holds a Master of Education as an Educational Diagnostician and a Bachelor of Interdisciplinary Studies, both from the University of Texas at El Paso. She is an international best-selling author and has been featured on the radio and in the media. Dr. Gonzalez has 20 years of experience in public education and currently implements a co-teaching model at the elementary level, providing bilingual, specialized curricular support to teachers and at-risk students. She has written curriculum for the school district where she is employed and facilitated district-wide professional development. Additionally, she has been an adjunct faculty member for the University of Phoenix since 2010. Dr. Gonzalez reaches high levels of success with both teachers and students by engaging in meticulous data analysis and taking an inclusive approach to implementing a universal design for learning that works for all students.

To reach Dr. Yvonne L. Gonzalez for information on academic support or guest speaking, please **e-mail: yvonne1615@sbcglobal.net**

Dr. Teresa E. Sanders has 20 years of experience in community mental health and has been an educator for 14 years. Dr. Sanders is the founder and owner of Safari Small Schools, a private pre-K through 3rd grade micro-school for students who aren't thriving in the traditional classroom setting. Dr. Sanders also contracts as a successful in-home teacher for students with significant behavior problems. Dr. Sanders provides support and training to parents and child(ren) simultaneously to restore order in the home and achievement in academics.

Dr. Sanders works successfully with diverse students and families taking a holistic, comprehensive approach to interpersonal interactions with parents and valuing them as allies in their children's education. She serves as an information outlet and advocate for students and their families, helping them make informed decisions about their children's education in and out of the public-school system.

Dr. Sanders lives in the small east Texas town of Canton. She is an international best-selling author, has been featured on the radio and in the media and writes education columns for four news outlets.

To reach Dr. Sanders for information on behavior consulting, academic services, or public speaking, please **email: TeresaESanders@gmail.com**

Dr. Cheryl Lentz is an international best-selling author, and keynote speaker, She holds a Doctor of Management Degree (DM) in Organizational Leadership, a Master of Science in International Relations from Troy University, and a Bachelor of Arts in Communication and Music History from the University of Illinois in Champaign, Urbana.

Dr. Cheryl, affectionately known as Doc C to her students, is a university professor of nearly 20 years, on faculty with Capella University, Embry-Riddle University, Grand Canyon University, and Walden University. Dr. Cheryl serves as a dissertation mentor / chair and committee member. She is also a dissertation coach, offering expertise as a professional editor for APA style for graduate thesis and doctoral dissertations, as well as faculty journal publications and books.

Awards include Walden Faculty of the Year, DBA Program, 2016, UOP community service award, Grand Canyon Outstanding Faculty Chair award November 2019, and 23 writing awards.

Dr. Cheryl is also an active member of Alpha Sigma Alpha Sorority.

She is a prolific author with more than 43 publications known for her writings on The Golden Palace Theory of Management and refractive thinking. Additional published works include her dissertation: Strategic Decision Making in Organizational Performance, Journey Outside the Golden Palace, The Consumer Learner, Technology That Tutors, Effective Study Skills, The Dissertation Toolbox, International Best Seller: The Expert Success Solution, and contributions to the award winning series: The Refractive Thinker®: Anthology of Doctoral Learners, Volumes I-XVII.

To reach Dr. Cheryl Lentz for information on refractive thinking, professional editing, or guest speaking, please visit her **websites: http://www.DrCherylLentz.com http://www.LentzLeadership.com** or e-mail: drcheryllentz@gmail.com

Index

A
Accountable care organizations (ACOs), 111–113
Advocacy, 37, 124
Agile, 2, 3, 9–13, 139, 143, 153, 159, 168
Agility, 132, 139
Algorithms, 8, 48, 49, 54, 55, 158, 160, 161
Artificial intelligence (AI), 5, 6, 8, 9, 13, 48, 50, 53, 132, 158

B
Business processes, 49, 84, 86

C
Care coordination, 111, 112, 114, 116, 120
Collective efficacy, 132, 139
Co-located teams, 2
Corporate culture, 29, 30, 74
Curriculum design, 183–185, 187–188, 190, 192–194
Characteristics, 8, 12, 28, 32, 141, 192
Collaboration, 3, 4, 10, 11, 48, 49, 71, 119, 124, 141, 193

E
Economics, 86
Educational, 183–187, 191, 194

Effective project management, 24, 37–39
Effective strategies, 33, 149
Emerging trends, 9
Emotional intelligence, 132, 142
Ensemble models, 49
Expert systems, 48
Explicit knowledge, 64

G
Group dynamics, 131, 132, 134, 139

H
Higher education, 56
Hiring, 8, 149–155, 158–161
Human resources, 3, 152, 158, 170
Hybrid delivery, 9, 12

I
Infrastructure, 29, 30, 35, 48, 50, 54, 55, 85, 101, 102, 114, 118, 167, 168

J
Joint finetuning, 48

K
Key performance indicator(s) (KPIs), 50, 118

Knowledge management, 63, 64, 66, 71–75, 78
Knowledge sharing, 63, 64, 66, 74–76, 78, 141
Knowledge transfer, 65, 67, 70, 74

L
Learner centric focus, 186, 194
Learning outcomes, 51, 187

M
Machine learning (ML), 47, 48, 55
Migration, 167, 168, 174

N
Neural networks, 6, 48, 49, 53, 55

O
Offshored, 85
Outsourcing, 83–97, 100, 101

P
PMBOK®, 65, 66, 68, 71, 142, 154, 161, 172
Polymorphic malware, 49
Population health management, 113, 114, 125
Problem, 4, 26, 75, 78, 83, 96, 100, 150, 154, 155, 168
Productivity, 7, 9, 10, 39, 99, 100, 133, 134, 136, 142
Project failure, 25–26, 37, 39, 131, 153

Project leaders, 24, 26, 28, 29, 32, 35–38, 74, 136, 137, 143, 153
Project management certifications, 175
Project Management Institute (PMI), 1, 28, 65, 131, 149
Project management tools, 1, 2, 6, 174
Projectized, 168, 169, 173, 176

R
Relocation, 85, 98–100, 174

S
Schedule, 6, 66, 68, 69, 72, 73, 78, 119, 133, 136, 150
Scope, 1, 10, 38, 63, 67, 69, 70, 117, 132–135, 150, 151, 169
Situational awareness, 132, 141
Situational leadership, 131, 137, 138, 143
Stacked neural networks, 48

T
Tacit knowledge, 64, 73, 75, 97
Tactical skills, 141
Task-oriented skills, 131, 138, 139
Team structure, 11
Triple aim, 112, 114, 123

V
Version one, 2

W
Waterfall delivery, 10, 12

The Refractive Thinker®

2020 CATALOG

The Refractive Thinker®:
An Anthology of Higher Learning

The Refractive Thinker® Press

info@refractivethinker.com
www.RefractiveThinker.com
blog: www.DissertationPublishing.com

Individual authors own the copyright to their individual materials. The Refractive Thinker® Press has each author's permission to reprint.

Books are available through The Refractive Thinker® Press at special discounts for bulk purchases for the purpose of sales promotion, seminar attendance, or educational purposes. Special volumes can be created for specific purposes and to organizational specifications. Orders placed on www.RefractiveThinker.com for students and military receive a 15% discount. Please contact us for further details.

Refractive Thinker® logo by Joey Root; The Refractive Thinker® Press logo design by Jacqueline Teng, cover design by Peri Poloni-Gabriel, Knockout Design (knockoutbooks.com), cover design & production by Gary A. Rosenberg (thebookcouple.com).

I think therefore I am.
—Renee Descartes

*I critically think to be.
I refractively think to change the world.*

Thank you for joining us as we continue to celebrate the accomplishments of doctoral scholars affiliated with many phenomenal institutions of higher learning. The purpose of the anthology series is to share a glimpse into the scholarly works of participating authors on various subjects.

The Refractive Thinker® serves the tenets of leadership, which is not simply a concept outside of the self, but comes from within, defining our very essence; where the search to define leadership becomes our personal journey, not yet a finite destination.

The Refractive Thinker® is an intimate expression of who we are: the ability to think beyond the traditional boundaries of thinking and critical thinking. Instead of mere reflection and evaluation, one challenges the very boundaries of the constructs itself. If thinking is *inside* the box, and critical thinking is *outside* the box, we add the next step of refractive thinking, *beyond* the box. Perhaps the need exists to dissolve the box completely. The authors within these pages are on a mission to change the world. They are never satisfied or quite content with *what is* or asking *why,* instead these authors intentionally strive to push and test the limits to ask *why not.*

We look forward to your interest in discussing future opportunities. Let our collection of authors continue the journey initiated with Volume I, to which *The Refractive Thinker*® will serve as our guide to future volumes. Come join us in our quest to be refractive thinkers and add your wisdom to the collective. We look forward to your stories.

Please contact The Refractive Thinker® Press for information regarding these authors and the works contained within these pages. Perhaps you or your organization may be looking for an author's expertise to incorporate as part of your annual corporate meetings as a keynote or guest speaker(s), perhaps to offer individual, or group seminars or coaching, or require their expertise as consultants.

Join us on our continuing adventures of *The Refractive Thinker®* where we expand the discussion specifically begun in Volume I: Leadership; Volume II (Editions 1–3): Research Methodology; Volume III: Change Management; Volume IV: Ethics, Leadership, and Globalization; Volume V: Strategy in Innovation; Volume VI: Post-Secondary Education; Volume VII: Social Responsibility; Volume VIII: Effective Business Practices in Motivation & Communication; Volume IX: Effective Business Practices in Leadership & Emerging Technologies; Volume X: Effective Business Strategies for the Defense Industry Sector; Volume XI: Women in Leadership; Volume XII: Cybersecurity in an Increasingly Insecure World; Volume XIV: Health care; Volume XV: Nonprofits; Volume XVI: Generations: Strategies for Managing Generations in the Workforce; and Volume XVII: Managing a Cultural Workforce: The Impact of Global Employees. All our volumes are themed to explore the realm of strategic thought, creativity, and innovation.

Dr. Cheryl A. Lentz, managing editor of The Lentz Leadership Institute, explains the unique benefits of the books for readers:

"They celebrate the diffusion of innovative refractive thinking through the writings of these doctoral scholars as they dare to think differently in search of new applications and understandings of research. Unlike most academic books that merely define research, The Refractive Thinker® offers unique applications of research from the perspective of multiple authors—each offering a chapter based on their specific expertise."

THE REFRACTIVE THINKER® PRESS

Volume I: An Anthology of Higher Learning

Volume II, 1st through 3rd Editions: Research Methodology

Volume III: Change Management

Volume IV: Ethics, Leadership, and Globalization

Volume V: Strategy in Innovation

Volume VI: Post-Secondary Education

Volume VII: Social Responsibility

Volume VIII: Effective Business Practices for Motivation and Communication

Volume IX: Effective Business Practices in Leadership & Emerging Technologies

Volume X: Effective Business Strategies for the Defense Industry Sector

Volume XI: Women in Leadership

Volume XII: Cybersecurity in an Increasingly Insecure World

Volume XIII: Entrepreneurship: Growing the Future of Business

Volume XIV: Health care: The Impact on Leadership, Business, and Education

Volume XV: Nonprofits: Strategies for Effective Management

Volume XVI: Generations: Strategies for Managing Generations in the Workforce

Volume XVII: Managing a Cultural Workforce: The Impact of Global Employees

Volume XVIII: Project Management: Strategies to Enhance Workflow & Productivity

Refractive Thinker volumes are available in e-book, Kindle®, iPad®, Nook®, and Sony Reader™, as well as individual e-chapters by author.

COMING SOON FROM THE REFRACTIVE THINKER®!
AVAILABLE THRU THE LENTZ LEADERSHIP INSTITUTE
The Refractive Thinker®: Vol XIX: Social Media

Telephone orders: Call us at 702.719.9214

- **Email Orders:** drcheryllentz@gmail.com

- **Website orders:** Please place orders through our website: www.RefractiveThinker.com

#1 INTERNATIONAL BEST SELLER!

The Refractive Thinker®: Volume XVIII: Project Management: Strategies to Enhance Workflow & Productivity

Join contributing scholars as they discuss doctoral research findings regarding the exciting field of project management. Doctoral scholars share current research and their words of wisdom regarding effective strategies project managers use to enhance workflow and increase productivity. Are you in the know regarding the most up-to-date strategies? Come join us! This volume will continue to shape the conversation of future success in business leadership around the world.

#1 INTERNATIONAL BEST SELLER!

The Refractive Thinker® Volume XVII: Managing a Cultural Workforce: The Impact of Global Employees

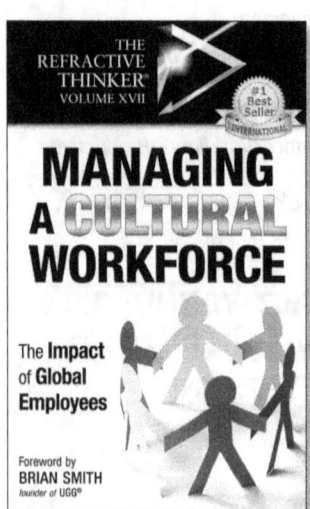

In this digital age, Americans (as well as citizens from countries around the world) now compete for jobs all over the globe. The digital age has opened borders in ways few imagined, presenting new challenges to leaders and stewards of companies as they embrace a multicultural workforce well beyond sovereignty and nationalism. Leaders, managers, and employees—all stakeholders—find themselves trying to unravel the challenges that multi-cultures from many countries bring to this global workforce.

For more information, please visit our website: www.RefractiveThinker.com

#1 INTERNATIONAL BEST SELLER!

The Refractive Thinker® Volume XVI: Generations: Strategies for Managing Generations in the Workforce

In this volume, join contributing scholars as they discuss research on effective management of multiple generations in the workforce, from Gen Z to Baby Boomers. The focus is on each of the generation's unique and diverse aspects pertaining to employment and management. This volume will continue to shape the conversation of their future success and examine proven strategies for continued excellence.

#1 International Best Seller!
2019 Next Generation Indie Book Awards® Finalist!

The Refractive Thinker® Volume XV: Nonprofits: Strategies for Effective Management

In this key volume, contributing scholars discuss research focused on nonprofit organizations and their specific needs regarding strategies for effective management. This volume continues to shape the conversation of their future success and the latest best practices and strategies for success.

For more information, please visit our website: www.RefractiveThinker.com

#1 Amazon Best Seller!
Next Generation Indie Finalist 2019
Gold & Silver eLit Awards 2019

**The Refractive Thinker®: Volume XIV:
Health Care: The Impact on Leadership, Business, and Education**

Dr. Gladys Taylor McGarey is internationally known for her pioneer work in alternative medicine. She believes that the practice of medicine has become a war against disease, a killing machine. Her premise is that we must change our focus from killing to living. As we support the living process in a person, life itself brings about the healing that the person needs. Our job as physicians is to work and support the 'Physician Within' each of us.

The Refractive Thinker®: Volume XIII: Entrepreneurship: Growing the Future of Business

Join Clarissa Burt and contributing scholars as they discuss current research regarding the future of business and the influence of the entrepreneur. This volume contains research on what the future may hold to success of the economy in the hands of the emerging and evolving small business owner and entrepreneur. As you read, ask yourself: "What should I be doing as an entrepreneur to contribute to the world economy as well as my own success?"

For more information, please visit our website: www.RefractiveThinker.com

PUBLICATIONS ORDER FORM

PLEASE SEND THE FOLLOWING BOOKS FROM THE REFRACTIVE THINKER®:
- ❏ Volume I: An Anthology of Higher Learning
- ❏ Volume II: Research Methodology
- ❏ Volume II: Research Methodology, 2nd Edition
- ❏ Volume II: Research Methodology, 3rd Edition
- ❏ Volume III: Change Management
- ❏ Volume IV: Ethics, Leadership, and Globalization
- ❏ Volume V: Strategy in Innovation
- ❏ Volume VI: Post-Secondary Education
- ❏ Volume VII: Social Responsibility
- ❏ Volume VIII: Effective Business Practices
- ❏ Volume IX: Effective Business Practices in Leadership & Emerging Technologies
- ❏ Volume X: Effective Business Strategies for the Defense Industry Sector
- ❏ Volume XI: Women in Leadership
- ❏ Volume XII: Cybersecurity
- ❏ Volume XIII: Entrepreneurship
- ❏ Volume XIV: Health care
- ❏ Volume XV: Nonprofits
- ❏ Volume XVI: Generations
- ❏ Volume XVII: Managing a Cultural Workforce

Please contact the Refractive Thinker® Press for book prices, e-book prices, and shipping. Individual e-chapters available by author: $3.95 (plus applicable tax). www.RefractiveThinker.com

- ❏ So You Think You Can Edit?
- ❏ The Expert Success Solution
- ❏ The Unbounded Dimensions Series
- ❏ Ethics, Employment Law, and Faith-Based Universities
- ❏ Effective Study Skills in 5 Simple Steps
- ❏ Technology That Tutors
- ❏ Siberian Husky Rescue
- ❏ The Consumer Learner
- ❏ Journey Outside the Golden Palace
- ❏ The Dissertation Toolbox

PLEASE SEND MORE FREE INFORMATION:
- ❏ Speaking engagements ❏ Educational seminars ❏ Consulting

JOIN OUR MAILING LIST:

Name: _____

Address: _____

City: _____ State: _____ Zip: _____

Telephone: _____ Email: _____

E-MAIL FORM TO: The Refractive Thinker® Press: drcheryllentz@gmail.com

Participation in Future Volumes of
The Refractive Thinker®

Yes, I would like to participate in:

❏ **Doctoral Volume**(s) for a specific university or organization:

Name: _____

Contact Person: _____

Telephone: _____ E-mail: _____

❏ **Specialized Volume**(s) Business or Themed:

Name: _____

Contact Person: _____

Telephone: _____ E-mail: _____

E-MAIL FORM TO: THE REFRACTIVE THINKER® PRESS
    drcheryllentz@gmail.com
    www.RefractiveThinker.com

- Join us on Twitter, LinkedIn, and Facebook

www.ingramcontent.com/pod-product-compliance
Lightning Source LLC
Chambersburg PA
CBHW070054110526
44587CB00013BB/1569